Academic Writing and Referencing for your
Social Work
Degree

CRITICAL STUDY SKILLS

Critical Study Skills for Social Work Students

Our new series of study skills texts for social work students has four key titles to help you succeed at your degree:

Studying for your Social Work Degree

Academic Writing and Referencing for your Social Work Degree

Critical Thinking Skills for your Social Work Degree

Communication Skills for your Social Work Degree

Register with **Critical Publishing** to:

- be the first to know about forthcoming social work titles;
- find out more about our new series;
- sign up for our regular newsletter for special offers, discount codes and more.

Visit our website at: **www.criticalpublishing.com**

Our titles are also available in a range of electronic formats. To order please go to our website www.criticalpublishing.com or contact our distributor NBN International by telephoning 01752 202301 or emailing orders@nbninternational.com.

Academic Writing and Referencing for your
Social Work
Degree

JANE BOTTOMLEY, PATRICIA CARTNEY AND STEVEN PRYJMACHUK

First published in 2018 by Critical Publishing Ltd

British Library Cataloguing in Publication Data
A CIP record for this book is available from the British Library

ISBN: 978-1-912096-23-7

This book is also available in the following e-book formats:

MOBI: 978-1-912096-22-0
EPUB: 978-1-912096-21-3
Adobe e-book reader: 978-1-912096-20-6

The rights of Jane Bottomley, Patricia Cartney and Steven Pryjmachuk to be identified as the Authors of this work have been asserted by them in accordance with the Copyright, Design and Patents Act 1988.

Text and cover design by Out of House Limited
Project management by Out of House Publishing
Printed and bound in Great Britain by 4edge, Essex

Critical Publishing
3 Connaught Road
St Albans
AL3 5RX

www.criticalpublishing.com

Paper from responsible sources

Contents

Acknowledgements

We would like to thank the many university and social work students who have inspired us to write these books. Special thanks are due to Anita Gill. Our appreciation also goes to Andrew Drummond and Maureen Finn for their comments on specific parts of the manuscript.

Jane Bottomley, Patricia Cartney and Steven Pryjmachuk

Meet the series editor and authors

Jane Bottomley

is the **Series Editor** for *Critical Study Skills* and a co-author of all the books in the series. She is a Senior Language Tutor at the University of Manchester and a Senior Fellow of the British Association of Lecturers in English for Academic Purposes (BALEAP). She has helped students from a wide range of disciplines to improve their academic skills and achieve their study goals. She has previously published on scientific writing.

Patricia Cartney

is Head of Social Work in the School of Health Sciences Division of Nursing, Midwifery and Social Work at the University of Manchester. She is a Principal Fellow of the Higher Education Academy. Her teaching and research interests focus on exploring how people learn best about professional practice and how they become knowledgeable and skilled social work practitioners.

Steven Pryjmachuk

is Professor of Mental Health Nursing Education in the School of Health Science's Division of Nursing, Midwifery and Social Work at the University of Manchester and a Senior Fellow of the Higher Education Academy. His teaching, clinical and research work has centred largely on supporting and facilitating individuals – be they students, patients or colleagues – to develop, learn or care independently.

Introduction

Academic Writing and Referencing is the second book in the *Critical Study Skills for Social Workers* series. The *Critical Study Skills for Social Workers* series supports student social workers as they embark on their undergraduate degree programmes. It is aimed at all student social workers, including those who have come to university straight from A levels, and those who have travelled a different route, perhaps returning to education after working and/or raising a family. The books will be of use both to students from the UK, and international students who are preparing to study in a new culture – and perhaps in a second language. The books also include guidance for students with specific learning difficulties.

Academic Writing and Referencing provides you with the knowledge, language, skills and strategies that you need in order to develop your academic writing skills and succeed in writing assignments. It introduces you to typical social worker writing assignments, and explores important areas such as the writing process, coherence, referring to sources, academic style and grammatical accuracy. It helps you to develop important skills such as planning and editing. It reflects the centrality of criticality in writing by referring to it throughout the different chapters, and shows how it is achieved through a multi-layered approach, including development of stance and argument, choice of language, and considered reference to sources. The book also helps you to prepare your work to a professional standard for submission.

Between them, the authors have many years' experience of social work, nursing practice and education, and academic study skills. All the information, text extracts and activities in the book have a clear social work focus and are often directly linked to the **Professional Capabilities Framework (PCF) and guidance from the Health and Care Professions Council (HCPC)**. There is also reference to relevant institutional bodies, books and journals throughout.

The many activities in the book include reflections, case studies, top tips, checklists and tasks. There are also advanced skills sections, which highlight particular knowledge and skills that you will need towards the end of your degree programme – or perhaps if you go on to postgraduate study. The activities often require you to work things out and discover things for yourself, a learning technique which is commonly used in universities. For many activities, there is no right or wrong answer – they might simply require you to reflect on your experience or situations you are likely to encounter at university; for tasks which require a particular response, there is an answer key at the back of the book.

These special features throughout the book are clearly signalled by icons to help you recognise them:

 Learning outcomes;

 Quick quiz or example exam questions/assessment tasks;

 Reflection (a reflective task or activity);

 Task;

Case studies;

 Top tips;

 Checklist;

 Advanced skills information;

 Answer provided at the back of the book.

Students with limited experience of academic life in the UK will find it helpful to work through the book systematically; more experienced students may wish to 'dip in and out' of the book. Whichever approach you adopt, handy **cross references** signalled in the margins will help you quickly find the information that you need to focus on or revisit.

There are four appendices at the back of the book which you can consult as you work through the text.

We hope that this book will help you to develop as an academic writer and to become a confident member of your academic writing community. We hope it will help you to achieve your goals and produce written work to the very best of your abilities.

Chapter 1
Academic writing:
text, process and criticality

Learning outcomes

After reading this chapter you will:

- understand what it means to be part of the academic writing community;

- be aware of the different text types you might need to produce as a student social worker;

- have developed an effective, systematic approach to the academic writing process;

- understand what it means to write critically;

- have learned about the foundations of different academic text types in social work, in particular, the critical essay.

Many aspects of your social work degree will be exciting and enjoyable. However, you will also face a number of challenges. You need to assimilate a great deal of information, and engage in new ideas and intellectual processes. What's more, you need to become proficient in academic writing, and learn how to produce the different types of text that are common in social work.

Academic writing is central to your university studies, as written assignments and exams will be one of the main ways in which you are assessed. This chapter explores the nature of academic writing in universities, and helps you to develop an effective, systematic approach to the academic writing process. All assignments are different, and universities vary slightly in terms of the types of writing assignments they employ. This chapter focuses on some general principles which can be applied to most academic writing, including what it means to write 'critically'. It also discusses some of the most common features of individual text types in your discipline, with a particular focus on the critical essay.

Academic writing at university: a new start?

Reflection

1) Do you enjoy writing? Why/Why not?

2) What kind of things have you written in the past (eg essays, reports, exams, articles, blogs, stories, poems)?

3) Do you have recent experience of writing academic essays? (If English is not your first language, were these in English or your first language?)

4) What comments have teachers or other people made about your writing in the past?

5) How do you feel about starting your first/next written assignment at university?

Social work students in the UK come from a range of backgrounds: some come straight from A levels (or Scottish Highers); some have been away from formal education for some time, maybe working and/or bringing up a family; some come from other countries to study in the UK. This means that students starting university may in terms of their current writing abilities, their experience of academic writing, and how confident they feel about tackling written assessments.

So where do you fit in?

You may be feeling confident. You may be relishing the prospect of writing your first assignment, seeing it as an exciting opportunity to explore your subject and demonstrate your knowledge and ideas. You may be able to draw on recent experience of academic writing and positive feedback from teachers.

Conversely, you may be feeling rather apprehensive about your first written assignment. Like many students, you perhaps see academic writing as one of the most difficult challenges of university life. There are a number of reasons why you may be feeling apprehensive. You might not have much experience of academic writing. Or maybe you do have experience, but it might have been a long time ago, or in your mother tongue, not English. You may have struggled with writing in the past and received some negative comments from teachers. All of these things can make the prospect of that first written assignment rather daunting.

CROSS REFERENCE

Chapter 2, Coherent texts and arguments, Editing and redrafting for coherence, The truth about writing!

When starting to write at university, it is important for students to draw on any strengths they have in terms of ability and experience. But it is also important for all students to identify aspects of their writing which can be improved on. At university, you are part of a **writing community**, comprised of students, lecturers and researchers, and all members of that community are constantly striving to improve as writers, even those who publish in journals and books.

You should commit yourself to improving as a writer throughout your degree programme, and beyond, in your professional life. It is not a question of achieving perfection; it is rather a case of committing yourself to making many small improvements over time, and not giving up when faced with a disappointment or hurdle. University lecturers see many students develop into very good writers after a shaky start. What these students have in common is a positive attitude, an ability to reflect on and critically assess their own work, and a willingness to seek and act on advice.

This book will support you in your development as a writer by helping you to approach writing in a systematic way. It will enable you to:

- analyse and respond to writing tasks;
- plan and structure your writing effectively;
- achieve clarity and coherence in your writing;
- produce writing which is accurate and academic in style;
- write critically in assignments;
- use and reference sources appropriately;
- prepare assignments to a high professional standard for submission.

This chapter sets you on your way by exploring the context of academic writing at university and providing guidance on how to approach writing assignments during your social work degree.

Academic writing for social work undergraduates

Undergraduate social work students may be asked to produce a number of different types of academic writing, including essays, written reflections, exams, reports, reviews of journal articles, and dissertations. This chapter sets out a general approach to academic writing that will help you with all types of assignments. It also provides specific information on essays, written reflections, exams and dissertations. Advice on practical writing tasks in social work is provided in *Communication Skills for your Social Work Degree*.

CROSS REFERENCE

Communication Skills for your Social Work Degree

- **Essays**. There are different types of essays. The main one, sometimes called a 'critical' or 'analytical' essay, requires you to explore a particular topic in depth, usually in response to a question or statement, and to explain your own viewpoint, or 'stance', supported by arguments and evidence. A 'reflective' essay requires you to analyse and evaluate a particular experience, explaining its impact on your understanding and future practice.

- **Written reflections**. Social work students are often required to produce short written reflections on their experience in practice, sometimes as part of a **portfolio** linked to their practice placements.

- **Exams**. In exams, you may be required to provide short or long written responses to questions or statements. These are usually designed to demonstrate that you have assimilated and understood the core work covered in a particular module. They may require you to recall factual information and/or to explain and support your viewpoint on a particular issue you have examined as part of your studies.

CROSS REFERENCE

Studying for your Social Work Degree, Chapter 6, Assessment

- **Dissertations**. A dissertation is a long evidence-based or research-focused essay written in the final year of your undergraduate studies.

Each of these types of academic writing will be discussed in more detail later in the chapter.

The writing process

Writing is a process and it involves a number of stages, including:

- 'unpacking' (analysing and understanding) the writing task and any guidelines provided;
- drawing up a provisional plan/outline;
- identifying relevant material that you need to read;
- reading and gathering information;
- drafting, redrafting, editing;
- revisiting and reworking your plan/outline;
- formatting your text;
- double-checking the assessment guidelines;
- proofreading.

It is important to fully engage with the writing process, and to understand that the *writing* process is part of the *learning* process. Writing is not just a question of getting fully formed thoughts down on paper (apart from in exams); it is a way of *clarifying your thinking* on a particular topic. Woodford (1967) put this nicely many years ago:

> The power of writing as an aid in thinking is not often appreciated. Everyone knows that someone who writes successfully gets his thoughts completely in order before he publishes. But it is seldom pointed out that the very act of writing can help to clarify thinking. Put down woolly thoughts on paper, and their wooliness is immediately exposed.

(p 744)

Top tips

CROSS
REFERENCE

Chapter 2,
Coherent
texts and
arguments,
Editing and
redrafting for
coherence

Engaging with the writing process

1) Try to develop good writing habits. Write little and often, especially if you have been away from formal education for a while.

2) Adopt a write-read-edit-read approach to writing (discussed in Chapter 2). When you stop to read what you have written, stand back from the text. Put yourself in the reader's shoes and make sure that everything hangs together, makes sense, and flows smoothly.

3) Try to get some feedback during the writing process. You may have the opportunity to submit a first draft to a lecturer, or you could ask a fellow student to read something and give feedback. If you do ask a friend or fellow student, it's a good idea to ask them to *summarise* what they think you are trying to say. If you only ask them if they understand what you have written, they may just say yes to be polite!

Your exact approach to the writing process will depend on the particular context of the assignment and your individual way of working, but some essential aspects of the writing process are discussed in the following sections.

Approaching a writing assignment

A writer needs an audience, a purpose, and a strategy, and these things are interconnected (Swales and Feak, 2012, p 10). When approaching a writing assignment, ask yourself:

CROSS REFERENCE

Analysing a writing assignment

- Who is reading my work? (your audience)
- Why am I writing? (your purpose)
- How will I achieve my purpose? (your strategy)

Your purpose is to meet the requirements of the assignment, and satisfy the needs and expectations of a particular reader. To determine your purpose, you need to analyse the wording of the task or question carefully. It may specify certain aspects of the topic that you should cover, and the verbs it uses, such as 'describe', 'explain', or 'evaluate', will determine how you treat this content. However, notwithstanding these specifications, there is no single 'right answer': different students will respond to a task in different ways. Your individual approach and strategy will determine:

CROSS REFERENCE

Appendix 3, Key phrases in assignments

- the selection of content (information, arguments, evidence etc);
- the way this content is structured and organised.

The person reading your essay must be able to discern *why* you have included particular content and organised your essay in the way that you have.

The question of the 'reader' is a tricky one. Of course, the actual human being reading your assignment is your university lecturer – probably the one who set the task and taught the module. However, lecturers often ask (or expect) you to imagine a 'hypothetical' or 'target' reader. This is usually someone with a similar level of knowledge to your own, or someone with a similar level of education but who is not an expert in social work. Lecturers want you to write for such a reader because they want you to *demonstrate* your understanding, and you cannot do this if you assume too much knowledge on the part of the reader. It is not uncommon to ask a student about something which is unclear in their essay, only to have them explain that 'the lecturer already knows this'! But this is not the point. The lecturer wants to know that *you* know this, and that you can explain it to other people, including non-experts, in a clear way. Always ask yourself:

CROSS REFERENCE

Chapter 2, Coherent texts and arguments, Editing and redrafting for coherence; Developing a coherent argument and expressing criticality

- What can the target reader be expected to know?
- What does the target reader need me to explain?

A good writer anticipates the reader's questions, and does not ask them to guess, fill in gaps, or work out how one thing relates to another.

Analysing a writing assignment

One of the most common – and perhaps surprising – reasons for low marks in written assessments is the failure on the part of the student to read the assignment title or question thoroughly enough. A student may go on to produce something which is interesting and of a good standard, but if they do not directly address the specific task, they will not meet the actual requirements of the assignment and so will end up failing. It is therefore essential to start any assignment by carefully analysing the assignment title or question.

CROSS REFERENCE

Appendix 3, Key phrases in assignments

You should read the title or question several times to 'unpack' it and get absolutely clear in your mind what is expected of you. It is helpful to highlight **key terms**, including verbs commonly occurring in academic assignments such as 'assess', 'discuss', and 'compare and contrast'.

Assignments usually come with a set of assessment **guidelines** and marking **descriptors** detailing the various criteria that you need to meet in order to achieve success. These criteria relate to areas such as:

CROSS REFERENCE

Studying for your Social Work Degree, Chapter 6, Assessment, Feedback on academic work

- task achievement;
- content and organisation;
- relevance to social work practice;
- writing style;
- referencing.

Be sure to read and digest these guidelines and descriptors as they are the very same ones that assessors will use to mark your work.

Task

Unpacking essay titles and questions

Look at the essay titles below. What are the key terms? What are you expected to do in your essay? What will be your purpose in writing? What type of content and organisation could help you to achieve this purpose? (Make some notes before you look at the model analyses provided.)

A

Given the many factors that might influence the future of a young person leaving the care system, consider the question, 'Can social workers really influence outcomes for young care leavers?'

B

'The core skill of social work is the ability to communicate.' Using appropriate evidence, explore the arguments for and against this proposition.

Discussion: unpacking essay titles and questions

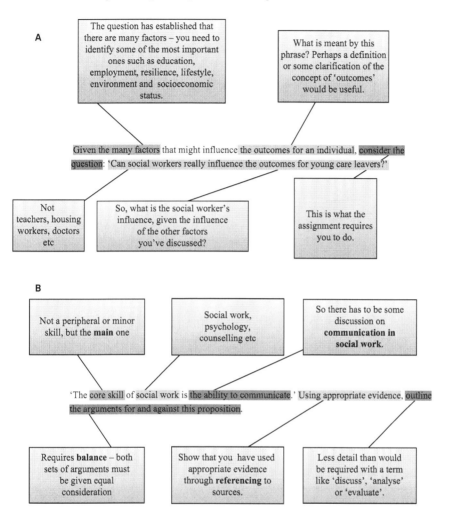

A

The question has established that there are many factors – you need to identify some of the most important ones such as education, employment, resilience, lifestyle, environment and socioeconomic status.

What is meant by this phrase? Perhaps a definition or some clarification of the concept of 'outcomes' would be useful.

Given the many factors that might influence the outcomes for an individual, consider the question: 'Can social workers really influence the outcomes for young care leavers?'

Not teachers, housing workers, doctors etc

So, what is the social worker's influence, given the influence of the other factors you've discussed?

This is what the assignment requires you to do.

B

Not a peripheral or minor skill, but the **main** one

Social work, psychology, counselling etc

So there has to be some discussion on **communication in social work**.

'The core skill of social work is the ability to communicate.' Using appropriate evidence, outline the arguments for and against this proposition.

Requires **balance** – both sets of arguments must be given equal consideration

Show that you have used appropriate evidence through **referencing** to sources.

Less detail than would be required with a term like 'discuss', 'analyse' or 'evaluate'.

Planning

Always begin an assignment by considering the constraints of the task: how long it should be and how long you have to write it. You could then draw up a provisional schedule which allocates time to the various sub-tasks. This schedule should leave sufficient time for you to read through and proofread the whole text several times before submitting.

A good piece of writing starts with a good plan or 'outline'. This should be primarily based on your analysis, or 'unpacking', of the task, but it should evolve as you engage in the reading and writing process. Your outline is therefore much more than a list of items related to the assignment topic: it is a developing conceptual representation of your response to the task. For example, in relation to the essay titles analysed above, your outline would reflect your position, or 'stance', in relation to the given topic, ie:

CROSS REFERENCE

Chapter 5, Preparing your work for submission, Editing and proofreading your final text

- A: the extent to which you believe, supported by your investigation of the arguments and evidence, that social workers can influence the outcomes for young care leavers

CROSS
REFERENCE

Writing
critically

- B: your assessment of the evidence you find to support or challenge the main proposition that communication is the core skill of social work

An outline should identify key sections of the text (with possible subheadings), and, in a critical essay, the arguments and evidence that would feature in each one.

CROSS
REFERENCE

Chapter 2,
Coherent
texts and
arguments,
Planning for
coherence

As discussed earlier in this chapter, different students will approach the same task in different ways. Sometimes an essay title will specify broad organisational requirements. For example, in B above, you are asked to 'outline the arguments for and against' the proposition. However, you might decide either to look at all the 'for' arguments in the first half of the essay and all the 'against' arguments in the second half, or, alternatively, to examine the proposition from both angles with reference to a series of different areas of social work. In other essays, you may have more leeway. One common approach is to examine different positions one by one, finally making a case for the one which the majority of the evidence seems to support. Another approach is to make a strong case for one particular position right from the start, while acknowledging and examining alternative (but in your view, weaker) viewpoints along the way.

Top tips

Aligning your outline and the task requirements

When your outline is well developed, go back to your initial analysis of the task to make sure that you have addressed all the points that you originally highlighted, and that you have achieved the required balance in your response.

CROSS
REFERENCE

Studying for
your Social
Work Degree,
Chapter 4,
Critical
thinking,
Applying and
developing
your critical
thinking skills;
Chapter 5,
Academic
resources:
technology
and the library,
The university
library

Reading and information gathering

Most academic writing assignments require you to read about a particular topic and use scholarly sources to inform your ideas. A good place to start the reading for an assignment is your lecture notes. These will provide an overview of the topic, and they will probably include links to some relevant literature, such as key chapters from core textbooks, and important journal articles, case studies, official reports etc. At the beginning of your studies, lecturers will tend to direct you to relevant sources in this way, but as you progress through your degree, you will be expected to explore the literature more widely and independently. As you develop these research skills, you will be increasingly assessed on your ability to find and select sources, and to use your critical judgement to assess their relevance and credibility. Lecturers will expect you to refer both to sources which support your position on a topic, and sources which challenge it.

Academic texts can at times appear long and difficult to read when you first approach them. It is essential that you devote enough time to reading, but it is also important that you develop effective reading strategies so that you use that time efficiently. When you approach a book, chapter or journal article, first adopt a 'global' approach, ie identify:

- what you expect to find out from it, and how these things relate to your assignment;
- the main message (the author's purpose in writing), and how this relates to your assignment;
- the main points made by the author(s), and how they relate to the main message of the article, and to your assignment.

As you think about how what you are reading relates to the assignment in hand, you might use highlighting, annotations, or note-taking to reflect this. You should also mark or make a note of parts of the text that you think you may need to read more closely at some stage.

Top tips

Strategies for effective reading

1) Use features such as contents pages, indices, abstracts, introductions and conclusions to help you assess the relevance of a book, chapter or article and find specific content.

2) Note how textbooks and journal articles on a particular topic are interrelated. Important books and articles are likely to be referenced by other scholars, and your initial reading may provide links to other sources that could be useful for your essay. This becomes more important as you progress in your studies.

3) You are likely to encounter unknown words in academic reading. Some of these might be subject-related terms, such as 'assessment' or 'intervention', which you should familiarise yourself with; others may be formal words which are uncommon outside academic writing, such as 'analogous' or 'dichotomy'. If English is not your first language, there may be quite a number of words which are new to you. There is a limited amount of time you can spend reading, so you need to make decisions about how much time to spend investigating unknown non-technical words. Looking up every word you don't know will eat into your reading time and disrupt the reading process. What's more, it is unlikely that you will be able to remember all of these words in the future. Try using these two questions to determine whether or not you should look up a word:

- Does the word prevent you from understanding the general meaning?
- Is the word repeated a lot in this text or related texts?

CROSS REFERENCE

Studying for your Social Work Degree, Chapter 4, Critical thinking, Active reading

If the answer to these questions is no, then attempt to guess the word using the context to help you, and read on; if the answer is yes, look up the word.

4) As you take notes, take care to make a note of the reference, including page numbers. It will waste a lot of time if you have to wade through all your sources again when you are compiling your list of references.

5) Try to paraphrase, ie take notes *in your own words*. This will benefit you in these ways:

- as you strive to express ideas in your own way, you will process them and get a good sense of how well you understand what you are reading;

- if you express things in your own words from the start, there is less of a risk of plagiarism in the final version of your assignment.

CROSS REFERENCE

Chapter 3, Referring to sources

Advanced skills

Understanding research article introductions: the CARS model

You will be expected to read and refer to research articles throughout your studies, but as you progress, you will be increasingly expected to take the initiative in finding and selecting particular articles that are relevant to your assignments. The first thing you should look at when considering an article is the **abstract**. This will give you a good idea of whether the article is useful and relevant. If you then decide that you want to find out more, you should begin by looking closely at the **introduction**. This will be easier if you know what to look for. Article introductions typically move through a series of rhetorical stages, or 'moves', ie parts of a text designed to have a particular effect; this is known as the CARS (Creating a Research Space) model (Swales, 1990, p 141).

- **Move 1** involves 'establishing a territory', ie showing that the research area is central or important. This is often achieved through a review of items of previous research in the area.

- **Move 2** involves 'establishing a niche', ie establishing an individual position in relation to the research previously conducted. This often means indicating a 'gap' in the research, by raising questions about or seeking to extend current knowledge in some way.

CROSS REFERENCE

Studying for your Social Work Degree, Chapter 3, Becoming a member of your academic and professional community, Academic phrasebank

- **Move 3** involves 'occupying the niche'. This can be by outlining the nature or purposes of the current research, announcing principal findings, and/or indicating the structure of the paper.

Awareness of the CARS model, and other typical rhetorical patterns, can help you to read and understand difficult articles. Furthermore, understanding the language associated with these rhetorical features of academic writing can help you develop your own academic writing 'toolkit'. You can find many examples of useful phrases which 'move a text forward' in the Academic Phrasebank:

www.phrasebank.manchester.ac.uk/

Writing essentials

There are three things which are especially important in academic writing.

1) **Relevance.** Be sure to make everything you write relevant to the task or question. If the relevance of a point is not immediately clear, then try to make it clear; if you cannot make it clear, leave it out. You will usually have a strict word count, so it is vital not to waste words on irrelevant material which cannot contribute to your mark.

2) **Coherence.** Lecturers often comment on the need for a piece of writing to be 'coherent', or deduct marks for 'lack of coherence'. To be coherent, a piece of writing must **make sense** to the reader. Coherence is tied up with issues discussed earlier, such as having a clear purpose and direction, and writing with a target reader in mind. It is also defined by clear organisation and expression. Coherent texts are *crafted*: they need careful planning and editing. The concept of coherence is examined in detail in Chapter 2.

CROSS REFERENCE

Chapter 2, Coherent texts and arguments

3) **Criticality.** Most academic writing is 'critical' writing, ie it is analytical and evaluative, rather than just descriptive. This will be discussed below and in other chapters.

CROSS REFERENCE

Chapter 2, Coherent texts and arguments, Developing a coherent argument and expressing criticality

Writing critically

A basic requirement in assignments is to make it clear that you have understood important concepts, theories and arguments. In your first year of study, this level of intellectual engagement and understanding is sufficient to pass an assignment. However, as you progress through your social work studies, you will be increasingly assessed on your ability to demonstrate that you have approached concepts, theories, arguments etc *critically*.

Stance

Criticality is related to the idea of having a clear **voice** (Argent, 2017). This means having something to say, and being in possession of an independent viewpoint or perspective on a given topic. In the academic world, this is known as your **stance**, ie, your position in relation to the topic (what *you* think about it) and to the reader (what you want *them* to think about it). There are two questions to consider:

CROSS REFERENCE

Chapter 3, Referring to sources

1) How can you explain your stance?

2) How can you justify your stance and persuade the reader that your stance is valid?

Consider the following essay title:

> Discuss the value of Cognitive Behavioural Therapy (CBT) in helping people experiencing depression.

Many people would be prepared to offer an opinion on this topic without thinking about it too much: 'I suppose psychological therapies must do some good, otherwise therapists, social workers and other helping professions wouldn't have a job!'; 'In my experience, people should just try and focus on things that make them happy and not worry about needing support from professionals.' Or they may be reluctant to voice an opinion: 'It's not something I've really thought about.' But your lecturers are not looking for this kind of response; they are interested in a viewpoint that emerges from your *critical engagement* with information, evidence, ideas and debate in academic literature, in this case, the literature dedicated to the issue of whether CBT is useful for people experiencing depression. *After carefully analysing and evaluating the literature*, you may come to the conclusion that a) CBT is of immense value in supporting people experiencing depression, b) CBT has little impact on people's experience of depression, c) CBT may have some value, in some circumstances, but other factors may impact equally or more – you may perhaps remain undecided in the face of conflicting evidence. These thoughtful conclusions are very different from the casual opinions stated at the beginning of this paragraph.

Argument

To explain and justify your stance to the reader, you need to present an **argument**. An argument is a way of organising and expressing a viewpoint. It involves a process of **reasoning**, and, to be valid in the academic world, it must be based on solid, convincing **evidence**. This will partly emerge from your analysis and evaluation of the stance, arguments and conclusions of other scholars, and of the evidence they use as support, according to objective criteria (Is the argument logical? Does it lead logically to their conclusions? Is the evidence sound? Does it support their claims?). You will need to compare alternative viewpoints and judge them according to the same criteria. It is on the basis of this analysis and evaluation that you will decide whether to accept the arguments, treat them with caution, or reject them. Your own argument can also be based on a more direct assessment of evidence. For example, you might look at a study on the impact of CBT and depression in Finland. You may decide that the findings and conclusions are convincing and widely applicable, or you may judge that the study is too small to be significant, or that it is only relevant to a particular social context.

It is not sufficient to look at facts, ideas and issues in isolation. You must demonstrate a good understanding of how these things interrelate. For example, you might compare and contrast several studies on the impact of CBT in helping people experiencing depression to determine if their findings are similar. If they are, this could provide powerful evidence to support a particular argument. If there are differences, you should try to find possible reasons for the differences. Could it be down to the different methodologies used, or are there other variables (eg age, gender, social context) which need to be taken into account? How do these facts impact on your own position?

Nuance

Students sometimes lack confidence in expressing their viewpoint in case it is 'wrong'. But your viewpoint is as valid as anyone else's, so long as it is supported with reasoned argument and sound evidence. However, being confident in your stance does not mean being rigid or close-minded. In fact, your stance should be **nuanced**. This means acknowledging strengths, weaknesses and grey areas. It entails, for example, sometimes *qualifying* your arguments or introducing *caveats* (CBT is often effective in helping people experiencing depression but for full benefits to occur service users do need to engage in considerable work outside of the sessions), or taking account of small but important differences in perspective (studies might have similar findings but interpret them in slightly different ways; two scholars may broadly agree that CBT interventions can benefit people experiencing depression but have different ideas about whether CBT should be used alone or whether it would be best to combine CBT with anti-depressant drugs to be most effective). A nuanced stance shows that you have been circumspect in your investigation and that you have not rushed to judgement. You must also be sure to recognise any limitations with regard to your own evidence, arguments or conclusions, and to clarify your position regarding which issues can be said to be resolved, and which remain open to debate.

Nuance is very important in social work essays which involve an examination of professional ethics and values. These are obviously complex issues, and it is expected that this complexity will be reflected in your discussion.

Expressing stance

Stance is conveyed through the way you treat your content, and through the way you organise and express your ideas. There are particular language features associated with the expression of stance (Biber, 2006; Argent, 2017). This will be explored through the task below, and in Chapter 2, where the organisation and expression of argument is explored in further detail.

CROSS REFERENCE

Chapter 2, Coherent texts and arguments, Developing a coherent argument and expressing criticality

Task

Writing critically

How is stance conveyed in the typical examples of student writing below? (Consider, for example, how the writers signal their analysis, evaluation, reasoning, interpretations, feelings and attitude.)

A

Research into psychosis has often focused on the role of the family. In the 1950s (when 'schizophrenia' was the more widely adopted term), the focus appeared to be on the family's role in the *causation* of psychosis. Consider, for example, Lidz et al's notion of 'pathological' families (1965) and the 'double-bind' hypothesis of Bateson et al (1956).

Around the same time as these 'causal' hypotheses were being promoted, the anti-psychotic drugs were discovered. Drugs, by their very nature, are treatments designated for the individual, and this fact, coupled with the prevailing view of families as toxic agents led, unsurprisingly, to what could cynically be called the first family intervention strategy – that of excluding the family.

B

One important element of communication in social work is *active listening*, whereby social workers fully concentrate on and reflect on what service users and carers say (Egan, 2014). According to Mobley (2005), active listening is an effective way of signalling empathy, as it conveys to an individual that they have the full attention of the person they are talking to. One aspect of active listening is verbal communication on the part of the listener, such as restating and summarising the speaker's message (Egan, 2014). Another important element of active listening is non-verbal communication. It is widely held that words form only a minor percentage of communication (Hargie et al, 2004; Sherman, 1993), and that a large part of any message is conveyed through 'paralanguage', such as tone of voice and intonation, and body language, such as posture, eye contact, facial expressions, gestures and touch (Argyle, 1988). This fact impacts considerably on the active listener, who not only has to be aware of the message conveyed through their own non-verbal communication, but also of any non-verbal cues from the speaker: 'One sigh may be communicating a lifetime of emotions' (Freshwater, 2003, p 93).

Discussion: writing critically

In these texts, examples of reasoning include:

- discussion of cause and effect

  This fact, coupled with the prevailing view of families as toxic agents **led**, unsurprisingly, **to** what could cynically be called the first family intervention strategy – that of excluding the family.

  This fact **impacts** considerably **on** the active listener.

- giving reasons for something

  Active listening is an effective way of signalling empathy, **as** it conveys to an individual that they have the full attention of the person they are talking to.

- exemplifying and explaining (in the third example, the colon introduces an elaboration of the point)

  Consider, **for example**, Lidz et al's notion of 'pathological' families (1965) and the 'double-bind' hypothesis of Bateson et al (1956).

  This fact, coupled with the prevailing view of families as toxic agents led, unsurprisingly, to what could cynically be called the first family intervention strategy – **that of** excluding the family.

  This fact impacts considerably on the active listener, who not only has to be aware of the message conveyed through their own non-verbal communication, but also of any non-verbal clues from the speaker: 'One sigh may be communicating a lifetime of emotions' (Freshwater, 2003, 93).

Analysis involves identifying relationships or patterns in the literature. This can be implicit in the organisation of ideas. In A, for example, notice how the writer, rather than just describing what each source says, uses his sources to exemplify a 'pattern' he/she has identified.

> Research into psychosis has often focused on the role of the family. **In the 1950s** (when 'schizophrenia' was the more widely adopted term), **the focus appeared to be on the family's role in the *causation* of psychosis. Consider, for example**, Lidz et al's notion of 'pathological' families (1965) and the 'double-bind' hypothesis of Bateson et al (1956).

Much analysis of the literature involves this 'drawing together' of ideas, or, as in the example below (from a journal article exploring the use of peer assessment as a way of enhancing learning for first year undergraduate social work students), comparing and contrasting different studies or 'threads' in the literature (in this case to illustrate how research studies have built upon ideas over a number of years to build an accumulated body of evidence), eg:

CROSS REFERENCE

Chapter 3, Referring to sources

> The landscape of higher education has undergone a series of major changes in recent years. A key transformation is how assessment is contextualised and understood. Assessment has been reconceptualised as not only measuring learning as an end product but also as a crucial factor in enabling – or preventing – learning to take place. Since the 1970s, an increasing amount of literature has highlighted the key role assessment plays in influencing student learning. Snyder (1971) initially drew attention to how assessment requirements dominate how and what students learn. Since then, this theme has been continually built upon by an increasing amount of pedagogic research and literature. Gibbs (1999) argued that assessment is the most powerful lever teachers have to influence student learning. Wass et al (2001: 945) highlighted that 'assessment drives learning … Pragmatically, assessment is the most appropriate engine on which to harness the curriculum'. Studies by Ramsden (1992), Boud (1995), and Black and Wiliam (1998), among others, all highlighted similar findings. Knowing that students tend to focus on what they need to do to successfully meet the assessment requirements for their studies is a major insight into where students channel their energies.
>
> (Cartney, 2010, p 551)

The texts in the task also include:

- language which indicates the writer's interpretation of or relationship with information and ideas in the literature ('has often focused on'; 'it is widely held that'; 'according to', which suggests a neutral stance towards the idea; 'appeared to be' and 'could be called', which suggest a cautious stance);
- language which suggests the writer holds a certain attitude towards information or ideas, and wishes to evoke a particular response in the reader ('by their very nature', 'unsurprisingly', 'cynically', 'important', 'considerably', and, in the Cartney extract above, 'major insight').

Stance can also be more subtly conveyed: the 'not only x but y' structure in Example B serves to indicate to the reader that the writer has identified 'y' (underlined) as the most important thing to focus on:

This fact impacts considerably on the active listener, who **not only** has to be aware of the message conveyed through their own non-verbal communication, **but also** of any <u>non-verbal cues from the speaker.</u>

Top tips

Summarising your argument

One way of developing and testing your stance is to see if you can write a single-sentence statement which you think summarises your argument. You can return to this statement as you read and write, and adapt it if necessary to reflect your changing thought processes. You may find that the final form of your statement ultimately forms part of your conclusion.

Task

Summarising your argument

Which of these statements represent **valid arguments** for the essay titles given below (and 'unpacked' earlier in the chapter)?

A

Given the many factors that might influence the future of a young person leaving the care system, consider the question, 'Can social workers really influence outcomes for young care leavers?'

Statement 1

Social workers can influence the outcomes of young people leaving the care system to some extent, but certain other factors such as the amount of additional support provided by extended family and friends and current employment/educational prospects tend to have a more significant impact.

Statement 2

It is not up to social workers to do too much for people. Individuals are responsible for their own lives.

Statement 3

Social workers should do more to help young people who are leaving the care system.

Statement 4

There are many factors which influence outcomes for young people leaving the care system, but social workers – acting on behalf of the local authority, who is the 'corporate parent' of a child in care – are strategically placed to have a significant impact on what happens to young people as they transition out of the care system.

B

'The core skill of social work is the ability to communicate.' Using appropriate evidence, explore the arguments for and against this proposition.

Statement 1

Social workers need to improve their communication skills as communication is the core skill of social work.

Statement 2

Communication is important but it is just one of many skills which are key to social work, some others being assessment skills and critical thinking.

Statement 3

Social workers require a variety of skills in their work, but the ability to communicate is the most important.

Statement 4

Social workers need a range of skills, including assessment skills and communication skills.

Discussion: summarising your argument

- Regarding Essay A, statements 1 and 4 are both valid arguments, as they recognise the premise that there are many factors influencing outcomes for young people leaving the care system, while also reflecting the emphasis in the essay title on the particular role of social workers. They convey different points of view, or stances, on how influential that role is (ie they have different interpretations of the literature, which they will need to justify), but this is to be expected. Statements 2 and 3 are just rather rash personal opinions, only loosely connected to the essay task.

- Regarding Essay B, statements 2 and 3 relate directly to the essay task, reflecting its clear focus on communication skills, even though they disagree on the relative importance of communication skills in comparison with other skills. Statements 1 and 4 are superficially related to the essay task, but they do not reflect the coverage or balance required.

The importance of evidence

To write critically, you need to be objective and able to distinguish between what is fact and what is theory or judgment. The more factual evidence you can collect to support theories, the sounder the arguments you will be able to make. This may be more complicated, however, than it initially appears. For example, even if we look across to the field of medical research we cannot be *absolutely* certain that smoking causes lung cancer or that HIV causes AIDS, but that is the way the bulk of the evidence currently points. In social work, 'evidence' is often not clear cut and needs contextualising. A professional judgement needs to be made as to whether or not the 'general' applies to the 'specific', ie does what the research suggests usually applies seem to apply in this case or not? You are entitled to have your own opinions, and you will not necessarily fail for disagreeing with current thinking (or, indeed, disagreeing with the views of your lecturers). However, you will almost certainly fail if you do not provide sufficient evidence (in the form of references) to back up your views. Social workers are expected to know the research evidence in relation to their areas of practice and to draw upon this evidence base when they make assessments and consider interventions.

The examples below contrast vague, overgeneralised or unsubstantiated statements with evidence-based claims.

> Social workers **are** generally happy with their pay and conditions. ✗

> A recent report (Department for Education, 2018) **suggests that** children and families' social workers are generally happy with their pay and conditions. ✓

> **It is a fact that** people experiencing mental health problems are more likely to be homeless. ✗

> **Recent evidence (eg Kelly, 2018) points to** a larger risk of people with diagnosed mental health conditions becoming homeless. ✓

> Research **has proved that** women are more likely to care for sick or elderly relatives than men. ✗

> Research **indicates that** women are more likely to care for sick or elderly relatives than men (Green, 2015). ✓

You can provide balanced arguments by comparing and contrasting evidence from different sources.

> There is little evidence to support a wholesale expansion of social work in cost terms alone. Thomas (2014), **however**, argues that the role preventive work plays in averting crises and high cost interventions should be calculated into any cost benefit analysis of social work costs.

> **Despite** government figures which suggest that social-care funding is at the highest level it has been since records began in the mid-1950s, Smith (2012) **maintains** that social care is grossly under-funded.

> **On the one hand**, social workers continue to report higher than average levels of job satisfaction (Dillon, 2016). **On the other hand**, there continue to be problems with retention of qualified staff in many parts of the UK (Department for Education, 2015).

Remember that not all evidence is equal. Be prepared to acknowledge when evidence is absent, unclear, contradictory, or not relevant to the current context.

Top tips

Putting ideas 'in the dock'

Try to think of academic arguments as a court case. You are a member of the jury and, before you make up your mind, you must listen to both the 'defence' (the arguments for) and the 'prosecution' (the arguments against). Hopefully, you wouldn't convict someone of a crime before listening to both sides and seeing what evidence is presented, so why believe unconditionally what academics have to say?

Writing essays

A critical essay is an in-depth exploration of a topic written in a formal style. The starting point for an essay may be a question for you to answer or a proposition for you to evaluate. Compare:

CROSS REFERENCE

Chapter 4, Language in use, Academic style

> How important is it for social workers to possess good communication skills?

> 'The core skill of social work is the ability to communicate.' Using appropriate evidence, explore the arguments for and against this proposition.

Essays involve discussion of theories and concepts which are key to your development as a social worker, and they often provide an opportunity for you to apply these theories or concepts to a real-world social work context.

Essay structure

Good essays have a structure to them – in simple terms, they have a **beginning**, a **middle** and an **end**. This resembles the narrative structure of novels and films, and in many ways, an essay is the 'story' of your investigation of a topic.

Introduction (the 'beginning')

CROSS REFERENCE

Appendix 4, Academic levels at university; Chapter 2, Coherent texts and arguments, Writing essay introductions and conclusions

The introduction 'sets the scene' of the essay, telling the reader what you are writing about and why it is important. In this section, you should explain how you propose to achieve your purpose in writing, ie how you will tackle the requirements of the essay title or question. You should provide some background information and outline the main concepts under discussion (providing clarifications and/or definitions if necessary). You should also include a brief outline which indicates the structure of the essay. The outline should reflect the actual ordering of information in the essay and relate directly to any headings and subheadings. This will help to make sure that you stick to the task in hand, and it will ultimately help the reader to navigate your essay. Aim to use approximately 20 per cent of your word limit for the introduction.

Main body of the text (the 'middle')

This part should form the bulk of your essay – as much as 60 to 70 per cent of your word count. It can be written as one large section, but the reader must be able to discern blocks of content relating to each subsection mentioned in your introductory outline (and smaller sections within this). You might find it useful to divide the text using appropriate subheadings. (Your department may have particular requirements with regard to this, so always check the assessment guidelines.) In the main body, you must meet the requirements of the essay title or question, according to the academic level you are expected to be at. So, for example, if you are asked to write a second-year (Level 5; Level 8 in Scotland) essay about the impact of CBT in helping people with depression (discussed earlier in this chapter), you will need to explore the arguments for and against the effectiveness of using CBT in this area. As many points of view as you can obtain must be taken into account, even if you don't agree with them – you are aiming to be as objective as possible.

Summary and/or conclusion (the 'end')

Summaries and conclusions shouldn't be more than about 10 to 15 per cent of your word limit. A summary expresses the main points of your essay in one or two paragraphs. It is not always necessary to have one, but it can be especially useful in longer (3,500+ word) essays. A conclusion usually refers the reader back to the introduction, to show you have achieved your stated purpose. It draws together the main points discussed in the body of the essay, and reiterates your stance. A conclusion allows you to make some decisions about the topic under discussion. At Level 5, for example, you have three options when concluding (as discussed earlier in this chapter): (i) you can come down in favour of the arguments for the issue being discussed ('CBT is a good way to tackle depression'); (ii) you can come down in favour of the arguments against the issue ('CBT does not seem to be an effective way of helping people experiencing depression'); or (iii) you can be a 'fence-sitter' and remain undecided in the face of conflicting evidence. All three options are equally acceptable, so long as your decision is backed up by appropriate evidence.

A **coherent** essay contains arguments which fit your position and lead naturally to your conclusion.

CROSS
REFERENCE

*Studying for
your Social
Work Degree,*
Chapter 3,
Becoming
a member
of your
academic and
professional
community,
The social
work
community

Reflective essays

A reflective essay, as the name suggests, is based on **reflection**. Reflection is the critical analysis of a situation or event, and of your own experience, perceptions, behaviour and thought processes. It can involve analysing situations and events that go well, or not so well. It is a way of making sense of your experience, and relating it to your wider studies and professional development, establishing meaningful connections between theory and practice. It is essential to the development of your knowledge, understanding and intellectual development. Reflection provides an opportunity to think deeply about your beliefs and attitudes, and to explore the values which underpin social work practice.

Reflective practice, the process whereby you stop and think about what you are doing on a day-to-day basis, is central to social work. It facilitates continuous learning in what is an ever-changing context.

Reflective essays revolve around an account of a particular event or experience in your practice, something that, on reflection, you view as a **learning experience**. This is known as reflection *on* action, ie looking back at something that has passed, as opposed to reflection *in* action, ie thinking about your current action (Schön, 1987) – though both are important in social work practice. Reflective essays are usually based on **reflective models**. One of the most well known of these consists of three simple questions (Borton, 1970):

- What?
- So what?
- Now what?

Another widely used model is Gibbs' Reflective Cycle:

CROSS REFERENCE

Studying for your Social Work Degree, Chapter 4, Critical thinking, Critical thinking in practice

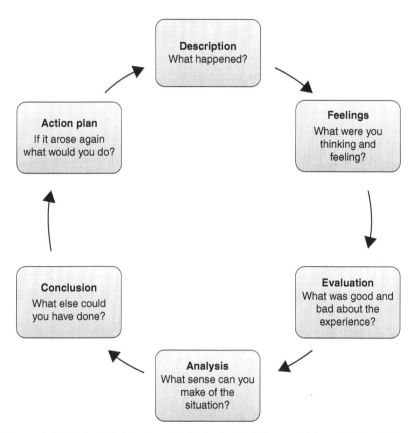

Figure 1.1: Gibbs' Reflective Cycle (adapted from Gibbs, 1988, p 50)

These reflective models provide a natural structure for a reflective essay.

- They first focus your thoughts on **what happened**, how you perceived an event or experience, and how you felt about it (Borton's 'What?'; Gibbs' 'description' and 'feelings'). This event or experience is commonly known as a **critical incident**, ie something that impacts on you in a significant way, either positively or negatively. Obvious critical incidents in life include the death of a loved one or the birth of your first child, but they can also be something more mundane (though still important in terms of your personal and professional development), like a difficult encounter with a colleague or service user.

- The models then focus on the **meaning** of the critical incident (Borton's 'So what?'; Gibbs' 'evaluation' and 'analysis'). Your critical analysis and evaluation of your experience should be informed by the literature, which can help you make sense of the issues which arise. So if, for example, you are writing a reflective essay on the first time you supported an older person moving from their home into residential accommodation, you would probably want to explore the meaning of 'home' to that person and to yourself. You would want to explore your own anxieties about loss and potential increased dependence both in relation to yourself and other members of your family. You might explore the literature around loss and bereavement to help you understand some of the emotions this move may be evoking – for both your service user and yourself. Bear in mind that when you explore this literature from a reflective standpoint you would be looking not just for information that helped you to describe social work practices but rather to compare and contrast your feelings and experiences with those of others. You would be seeking increased self-awareness and looking for a way of understanding and managing your emotions.

- The final consideration covered by the models is **action**, ie how different courses of action might have played out, what you might do if a similar situation arose in the future (Borton's 'What now?'; Gibbs' 'conclusion' and 'action plan'). This comprises an assessment of the impact the experience has had on your understanding and future practice, detailing any insights you have gained, and any actions you need to take in order to enhance your personal development or professional practice.

You might find that you are provided with a template by your programme or module lecturers to help you reflect, based on the above models. Alternatively, you might find it helpful to create a template of your own, perhaps based on a reflective model you like.

Reflective essays are, like other essays, formal in style. However, check assessment guidelines for information on, for example, the use of tenses and personal pronouns. You will usually need to use a range of tenses, for example, the past tense to describe the incident, the present to discuss your current beliefs, and the future to report future planned action. It is also often necessary or natural to use personal pronouns in a reflective essay, eg:

I noticed that Mrs A was crying.

I wondered how best to ask Mrs A what was distressing her.

However, where personal pronouns are rather 'chatty', and are easily replaced, it is better to avoid them, eg:

I thought Darren was frustrated. ✗

Darren appeared to be frustrated. ✓

I know I need to find out more about the benefits Mr N may be entitled to claim. ✗

It is clear that I need to find out more about the benefits Mr N may be entitled to claim. ✓

Top tips

Writing reflectively

1) Reflections are personal, but try to put some distance between you and the critical incident so that you can evaluate it as objectively as possible. Your objectivity should be reflected in your tone, which should be calm, restrained, and factual, eg 'the social worker confronted the parents about their child's poor school attendance and the teachers in the room appeared uncomfortable' rather than 'the social worker spoke about the child's poor attendance and this made the teachers wish they weren't in the room'.

2) Don't make assumptions and be cautious in your assessments. It is difficult to judge a situation when you have limited information. You cannot usually be sure why someone is behaving in a particular way, but you can speculate, eg 'she *seemed* anxious, *perhaps* because she was uncomfortable with the situation'.

3) Do not confuse your perception with fact, eg 'she *came across as* a bully' rather than 'she *is* a bully'; 'he *appeared to have* dementia' rather than 'he *clearly had* dementia'.

4) Be respectful in the way you refer to people, eg 'an *elderly* woman' rather than 'an *old* woman'; 'a young adult with a suspected eating disorder' rather than 'an anorexic girl'.

5) Anonymise participants. This can be done by using official titles ('the senior practitioner') or pseudonyms.

Task

Reflective essays

Which section of a reflective essay do you think the following extracts come from? What tells you this? Can you relate them to the reflective models discussed above?

A

Aisha (a pseudonym), a 22-year-old young woman, came to the drop-in session at your practice placement. She recently found out that she is three months pregnant and she came to say that she has been experiencing panic attacks since. She said she did not know what to do about the baby and she felt this was making her feel her life was out of her control.

B

Seeing Aisha in a state of turmoil and distress made me worry about how I could best help her. I was very concerned that I might end up saying the 'wrong' thing to her. I have strong feelings about terminations and I was worried I might convey these feelings to Aisha inappropriately and make her feel worse. I felt unsure how to manage a conflict between my personal and professional values and how I could manage my emotions so I could work with Aisha to help her make the right decision for her – even if this was not the same decision I would have made in her situation.

C

I discussed my feelings with my Practice Educator in supervision that afternoon. My Practice Educator was very understanding and appreciate my concerns. She encouraged me to explore my feelings more and helped me to separate out what I felt from what I thought Aisha may have felt. Through engaging openly in this discussion I was able to analyse my feelings more deeply and I managed to separate out my personal values from my professional values. Focusing on Aisha's right to self-determination and the importance of helping her make her own decision was a helpful process.

D

Following the discussion with my Practice Educator, I found I was able to work with Aisha in a very professional way when we next met. I was more able to manage my own value conflict and to prioritise supporting Aisha to make her own decision. I had been able to separate out what feelings belonged to Aisha and what feelings belonged to me. When I wrote up this learning experience in my weekly learning log I was able to offer it as an example of how I had met some of the requirements of the Professional Capability Framework in relation to Values and Ethics. I was able to show how I had been able to manage the impact of my own values on my professional practice and how – with support – I had effectively managed to deal with a situation of value conflict.

Writing short reflections for journals or portfolios

You may also be required to submit short written reflections (approximately 300–1,000 words) for assessment as part of your social work degree (distinct from the 'reflective essay' discussed previously in this chapter). Reflective writing sometimes permeates whole course units, or even entire programmes of study, via a **reflective diary** (also known as a **reflective journal** or **reflective log**) that requires regular entries.

As with a reflective essay, a mixture of tenses is used as you move between past, present and future. However, in contrast to an essay, the writing style used in reflective accounts in journals or for portfolios can be relatively conversational, and the first person pronoun ('I') is almost always used.

Task

Reflective writing

1) Look at the piece of reflective writing below. What do you notice about the following?

- the style of writing;
- the use of tenses;
- the relation to the reflective models (Borton, Gibbs) discussed in the previous section.

During my placement I visited a residential home for older people. I went to talk to a man because he looked like he was upset. I asked him his name but he just snapped and told me to get lost and mind my own business. He was the same when his wife came in. It upset me a bit but I wondered if everything was OK with him so I asked my Practice Educator when we had supervision. She explained that the staff thought he may have dementia and that this sort of behaviour was common in people with undiagnosed dementia and that I shouldn't take anything personally. I did some reading on dementia after my visit and it made me understand why he might be behaving in the way he was. I will talk to my Practice Educator again tomorrow to see if she has any tips or advice on how I might be able to communicate with him better.

2) Compare the two reflections, A and B, below. What are the main differences? Which one is not acceptable and why?

A

I had real difficulties whenever I accompanied Mrs Evans to the Housing Department at Cheetham Brow. One of the Housing Officers there, Mrs Laddell, was a real bully. She used to pick on people and shout at them. Mrs Evans had been recently bereaved and was trying to readjust her benefits to cover her housing costs. Mrs Laddell implied she was stupid because she didn't understand how to complete the eight-page Change of Circumstances form. She was even worse to the person in front of us as she told him that he would be able to pay his rent if he spent less on buying expensive trainers. I have got a pair of the same trainers and they are on sale on the market for £7.99! I told my Practice Educator about this in my last supervision and she said I should ring up the Housing Department to complain. I was really nervous about doing this and I think maybe my Practice Educator should really have rung herself as I am just a student. When I rang though the manager there was really nice and said she would talk to Mrs Laddell about her attitude.

B

I had real difficulties when I accompanied Mrs Rodgers (a pseudonym) on her visits to a local Housing Department. One particular day I was especially distressed as a Housing Officer was rude to the service user I was supporting and another young person who was trying to sort out his rent arrears. I was concerned that her attitude was very judgmental and left both Mrs Rodgers and the other tenant, who was seen before us, feeling embarrassed and demeaned. At the time I felt too nervous to say anything as I was afraid I would say the wrong things and I would end up making people more rather than less embarrassed.

I reflected further on this however and raised the incident in supervision with my Practice Educator. My Practice Educator encouraged me to contact the manager of the Housing Department directly to express my concerns. I did so and the manager appeared very grateful for my feedback. She said she herself had been concerned about the culture that had started to develop within the office. She explained staff all had additional responsibilities and people who left were not being replaced. She said this led to some staff feeling stressed and overworked. She did not condone rude behaviour, however, and said she would speak with the member of staff involved and advise her about how service users are to be treated with respect at all times. The manager said she would run a training programme on customer care and invited Mrs Rodgers and myself to be part of planning this.

This episode helped me to realise that it is not too late to raise concerns after the event even if it seems too difficult to do so as they are happening. I also realised that it is good practice to bring concerns to the attention of appropriate people and that this may change future practice.

Discussion: reflective writing

1) The reflection mostly follows the reflective models (Borton, 1970; Gibbs, 1988) discussed earlier in the chapter: the writer describes the critical incident, and her feelings about it, and there is some analysis of the wider issue, ie the reasons behind the incident; she also describes the action she has taken to help understand the illness better, and indicated future action, ie seeking advice from her Practice Educator. The style is relatively conversational, there are informal expressions ('get lost', 'mind my own business', 'upset me a bit'), and the first person ('I') is used throughout. However, it is not overly chatty or in any way inappropriate – in fact, it is **restrained** and **thoughtful** ('upset me a *bit*', 'I *might*'). The **critical incident** is related **calmly** and **factually**. It is clear that the student has understood the **value of reflection** and the nature of the **learning process**. The 'narrative' is related in the past tense ('she treated', 'I contacted'), present tense is used for facts ('is behaving'), and future is used for planned action ('I will talk').

2) Reflection A describes a critical incident, but it is related in a rather clumsy, judgemental fashion, and where there should be analysis, there is only really a description of what happened. The student does not seem to have learned anything useful from the incident, and there is very limited reflection on her feelings or any attempt to understand why the situation may have occurred in the way it did. Reflection A is also clearly problematic in terms of confidentiality because it names the place and the people involved directly.

Reflection B is much better. The language used to relate the critical incident is much more **cautious** and **restrained**. The analysis of the incident is **calm** and **factual**, and sensible future action and future learning have been identified. The participants are not identifiable. They are referred to in a general sense rather than by name.

Writing in exams

Examinations test your ability to recall information and write under pressure. However, as with any written assignment, you should read the question or task carefully and highlight key words. You can use the exam booklet to jot down basic ideas and outlines, as long as you cross out any rough work before handing it in. In exams, you do not have a lot of time to spend thinking about organisation, expression or presentation, and examiners will take this into account. Nonetheless, whatever you can do to make the examiner's life easier will count in your favour – remember, your exam script may come from the middle of a pile of 200 or more!

Top tips

Exam strategies

- In a long answer, stick to one point per paragraph and leave a line between paragraphs. This will make your exam script easier to read.
- Make your handwriting as clear as possible – you can get no credit for ideas if no one can read them.
- Make it clear which question you are answering.

Assessment task

Answering exam questions

Look at the exam question below and the students' answers. Have they answered the question well? Why/why not?

'Social work that is not relationship-based is not really social work'. Discuss.

Answer A

Effective social work involves a combination of knowledge, values and skills. A social worker needs to have knowledge (eg knowing about the law, policies, research and theories) and intellectual abilities (eg critical thinking and problem solving). They also need to have skills (eg knowing what questions to ask in an assessment and how to present information professionally). Social work is also about values, however, and seeking to form an empathic and trusting relationship with the person the social worker is engaging with is key to what social work is. It is about more than knowing and doing; it is about being and how people are treated. The Munro Review of Child Protection (2011) powerfully raised concern about an over-bureaucratised, target-driven system where the centrality of social workers forming relationships with children and families, in order to understand and help them, had become obscured in a compliance culture. Munro encouraged the profession to hold relationship-based practice as central and to move from a compliance to a learning culture.

Answer B

Social work needs to be relationship-based. The Munro Review (2011) said that social workers were not forming relationships with children and families. We need to do something about that. My Practice Educator said I form good relationships with colleagues and service users and carers. I am pleased about that. If I didn't I would not really be doing social work as the essay title suggests.

Discussion: answering exam questions

- Answer A situates the discussion question in a clear context and provides an independent point of view, supported by examples, and an appraisal of wider implications.
- Answer B does not answer the question. It states facts without offering any analysis. Many statements are unsubstantiated or purely anecdotal. It meanders from point to point, and the style is rather informal and chatty.

Writing dissertations

A dissertation is a long evidence-based or research-focused essay, usually between 10,000 and 20,000 words. It shares many of the requirements discussed in relation to critical essays, such as having a clear purpose and strategy, a defined target reader, a conventional structure, and a well-developed stance and argument. An **evidence-informed** social work dissertation could involve conducting your own review of the evidence surrounding a particular area of social work practice. A **research-focused** dissertation could involve investigation of a current 'knowledge gap' or 'problem' in the field of social work. However, because of the strict ethics associated with conducting research, undergraduate social work students tend not to do research-focused dissertations (though this is an expectation of many postgraduate dissertations).

Before you start your dissertation, you will have to write a **proposal** outlining your chosen line of enquiry. You will need to make it clear that the dissertation is feasible, and that you have the knowledge and skills to carry it out. You will also need to outline any potential challenges or problems you foresee. With research dissertations, you will need to complete the ethics form prescribed by your university. Finally, you will need to include an initial bibliography, ie sources that you think will be of use to you.

Like all essays, dissertations must have a 'beginning', a 'middle' and an 'end'. An **introduction** provides background information on the topic under review, or the gap or problem under investigation. The introduction also presents the rationale for your current review or investigation, and outlines how you intend to go about your study. A **conclusion** serves to draw everything together with a summary of the main argument and its implications for social work practice.

The 'middle' part of a dissertation is founded on an extensive **literature review**, presenting an analysis and evaluation of current scholarship on the topic, and detailing key concepts, theories and arguments.

Research-focused dissertations may adopt the following structure:

- Introduction;
- Legislation and Policy Context;
- Literature review;
- Theory;
- Method;
- Results;
- Discussion;
- Implications for practice;
- Conclusion.

With this structure, the **introduction** sets out what the work is aiming to achieve and provides an overall summary of the following chapters. This is often followed by a chapter outlining the **legislative and policy context** of the topic you are studying. Next is a **literature review** chapter which highlights the key themes identified by literature and research as being most important in this area. You may also be asked to write a chapter which draws explicitly on one or more social work **theories** and discusses the application of these ideas to your study. Your **methodology** describes the type of study you are conducting (quantitative, qualitative, mixed methods), and your methods of data collection and analysis (eg semi-structured interviews, surveys or focus groups). It also covers any ethical considerations. The **results** section details the findings of your study and highlights the key messages from your research. The **discussion** section is where you interpret your findings and discuss their meaning and significance. This will involve relating what you have found out to current knowledge in the field, and highlighting any new insights or understanding. You will also be expected to directly address what you think the implications of your study suggest in relation to implications for practice. You might make some recommendations for changes to future social work practice as a result of your findings. You will tie your work together in a concluding chapter which summarises your research process and findings and draws the work to completion.

Dissertations also have an **abstract**, which comprises a short summary of the whole dissertation, and a list of **references**.

CROSS REFERENCE

Studying for your Social Work Degree, Chapter 3, Becoming a member of your academic and professional community, Academic principles, pursuits and practices, Teaching, research and knowledge

CROSS REFERENCE

Studying for your Social Work Degree, Chapter 3, Becoming a member of your academic and professional community, Advanced skills, Research reports

Summary

This chapter has introduced the topic of academic writing. It has explored the context of academic writing at university, and provided guidance on how to approach academic writing tasks in your social work degree. It has explored some of the general principles of academic writing, the writing process, and important features of typical text types in social work. It has also highlighted the centrality of criticality in writing, something which will be expanded on in subsequent chapters.

Sources of example texts

Cartney, P (2010) Exploring the Use of Peer Assessment as a Vehicle for Closing the Gap between Feedback Given and Feedback Used. *Assessment and Evaluation in Higher Education*, 35(5), 551–64.

References

Academic Phrasebank. [online] Available at: www.phrasebank.manchester.ac.uk (accessed 15 February 2017).

Argent, S (2017) The Language of Critical Thinking. [online] Available at: www.baleap.org/event/eap-northcritical-thinking (accessed 27 February 2017).

Biber, D (2006) Stance in Spoken and Written University Registers. *Journal of English for Academic Purposes*, 5(2), 97–116.

Borton, T (1970) *Reach, Touch and Teach: Student Concerns and Process Education*. London: Hutchinson.

Gibbs, G (1988) *Learning by Doing: A Guide to Teaching and Learning Methods*. Oxford: Further Education Unit, Oxford Polytechnic.

Munro, E (2011) *The Munro Review of Child Protection: Final Report A Child-centred System*. London: Department for Education.

Social Work Reform Board (2012) Professional Capabilities Framework. [online] Available at www.basw.co.uk/resource/?id=1137 (accessed 7 February 2018).

Schön, D (1987) *Educating the Reflective Practitioner: Towards a New Design for Teaching and Learning in the Professions*. San Francisco: Jossey-Bass.

Swales, J (1990) *Genre Analysis*. Cambridge: Cambridge University Press.

Swales, J and Feak, C (2012) *Academic Writing for Graduate Students: Essential Tasks and Skills.* 3rd ed. Michigan: Michigan ELT.

Woodford, P (1967) Sounder Thinking Through Clearer Writing. *Science*, 156(3776), 743–45.

Chapter 2
Coherent texts and arguments

Learning outcomes

After reading this chapter you will:

- have gained an understanding of the concept of coherence in writing;

- understand the importance of effective planning;

- understand how to write effective essay introductions and conclusions;

- understand the importance of editing and redrafting your text;

- understand how to develop paragraphs and texts which are easy to follow for the reader;

- understand how to develop coherent arguments;

- be aware of how your choices of grammar and expression can affect meaning, clarity and coherence.

Reflection

1) What do you think it means to write 'coherently'? How do you think this can be achieved?

2) What do you understand by 'a coherent argument'? How is a coherent argument constructed?

3) How do you go about planning a piece of written work? How much time do you spend on this?

4) How do you go about editing a piece of written work? How much time do you spend on this?

If a text is **coherent**, it **makes sense to the reader**. In this chapter, you will analyse a range of academic social work texts to help you understand how coherence is achieved. Alongside this, you will develop effective planning, writing and editing strategies so that you are able to produce coherent texts and arguments of your own.

Planning for coherence

Planning is the process of selecting and organising information and ideas in order to respond to an assignment task effectively. The planning process should start with an examination of the wording of the task or question. This involves analysing – or 'unpacking' – it so that you can be sure about what the lecturer assessing your work is expecting you to do.

When you are sure you understand what you are being asked to do, you should start to draft a plan or 'outline'.

An outline is much more than a mere list of topics; there should be a clear **organising principle**, both for the text as a whole, and for individual sections of the text. This might involve presenting items chronologically, or in order of importance; it often involves starting with general information and moving on to more specific information. Your outline should indicate how individual items relate to the main topic and to each other, ie how they are governed by your main organising principle.

Below are some examples of common organisational frameworks (for a piece of writing, or for sections of a piece of writing) which can help you to organise information and ideas (Jordon, 2001):

- **classification**, ie the division of something into groups, classes, categories etc, usually according to specific criteria;

- **comparison and contrast**, ie an examination of similarities and differences;

- **cause and effect**, ie how one thing influences another; what results from certain situations or actions;

- **problem-solution**, ie the description and analysis of a problem, and the evaluation of possible solutions to that problem.

Other common elements of academic texts include **description**, **narrative**, **definition of key terms**, and **exemplification**. These different elements may overlap: there is likely to be discussion of the causes and effects of a problem; classification may well require discussion of similarities and differences; description, definition of key terms, and exemplification are integral to many organisational frameworks.

CROSS REFERENCE

Chapter 1, Academic writing: text, process and criticality, Analysing a writing assignment

CROSS REFERENCE

General and specific information

Task

Organisational frameworks

1) What organisational principles are being employed in the essay plans below?

A

Factors that might influence a young child's development

- diet, eg nutritional requirements met or not met

- environment, eg house is safe, no hazards

- stimulation, eg opportunity to play, develop and learn

- socio-economic status, eg poor housing, damp etc

- cultural factors, eg child rearing practices and expectations of child behaviour

- health practitioners, eg GPs, nurses, midwives

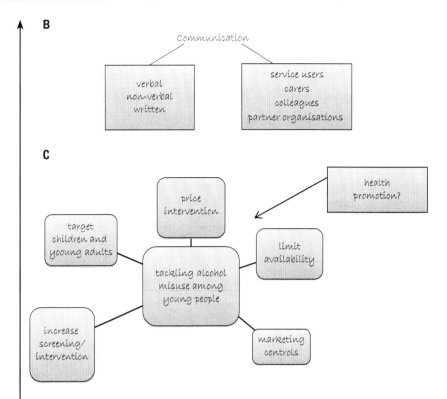

B

Communication

verbal
non-verbal
written

service users
carers
colleagues
partner organisations

C

price
intervention

health
promotion?

target
children and
yooung adults

limit
availability

tackling alcohol
misuse among
young people

increase
screening/
intervention

marketing
controls

D

Women's experience of being HIV-positive in pregnancy (Lingen-Stallard et al, 2016)

- shock and disbelief
- anger and turmoil
- acceptance and resilience

E

- Researchers from the Institute for Fiscal Studies, Harvard University and the University of Cambridge found that the median earnings of English women with degrees ten years after graduating were three times higher than women who were not graduates (www.ifs.org.uk/publications/7998)
- Graduating from university appears to be financially advantageous for women
- Look at how to increase the number of women entering degree courses eg via a targeted recruitment drive?

F

Should young people be given antidepressants? (Kendal and Pryjmachuk, 2011)

COTGROVE, 2007	TIMINI, 2007
- cites studies that show benefits (NCCMH, 2005; Whittington et al, 2004) - claims alternative therapies such as CBT, interpersonal therapy and family therapy have limited effect	- questions evidence - believes most childhood distress is self-limiting and does not require extensive intervention - believes marketing spin has taken precedence over scientific accuracy - claims link between antidepressants and suicide

2) Which of the sections below do you think are relevant to the essay provided? How could the relevant sections be effectively organised?

A

Given the many factors that might influence the future of a young person leaving the care system, consider the question: 'Can social workers really influence outcomes for young care leavers?'

Introduction/background – refer to title

- Factors influencing outcomes for young care leavers (presence or absence of support networks, whether in education/employment, physical and mental health (current and past), whether there is evidence of the young person developing resilience)
- Definition of social worker and explanation of role of social work with young people leaving the care system
- Definition of outcomes
- Definition of influence – for good and ill
- Link with legal and policy frameworks
- Extent to which social workers can influence – barriers and opportunities
- Compare with influence of others, eg foster parents, teachers

Conclusion – can have an impact, but other factors (eg presence of support networks, employment, education etc) have more – potential of social workers to influence these things? May be that social workers influence outcomes through their relationships and direct work with young people. May also be via social workers helping young people work more on the factors most likely to have an impact on their outcomes, eg to engage with people, apply for jobs and/or educational courses.

B

'The core skill of social work is the ability to communicate.' Using appropriate evidence, explore the arguments for and against this proposition.

Introduction/background – claimed that communication is the <u>core</u> skill of social work

- Definition of communication
- Definition of proposition
- Relative importance of (other) different core skills , eg problem solving skills, organisational skills, prioritising workload, having good time management – less important than communication?
- All social workers should learn how to work most effectively with interpreters
- Problems caused by breakdown in communication (often noted in Serious Case Reviews which are undertaken when a child dies or is seriously harmed as a result of abuse or neglect)
- Problems caused by poor communication with service users and carers
- Service users and carers rating the ability to communicate well as a key social work skill
- Problems caused by poor communication across professions (different disciplinary starting points)
- Different types of communication: verbal, written, non-verbal
- How communication impacts on other aspects of social work – thus more important?
- Different forms of communication: service users and carers, colleagues, other professional organisations

Conclusion – social workers need a range of skills but communication is integral to all, and very difficult to be a good social worker without good communication skills, even if competent in other skills

Editing and redrafting for coherence

Editing is a process whereby a writer makes changes to the content, organisation and expression of a text in order to improve it. The writing and editing process is also referred to as 'drafting' and 'redrafting', with writers producing different 'drafts' of a text. (Lecturers may sometimes ask you to submit 'a first draft' – though this does not mean that it should be unedited! It is probably best to think of this as 'an early draft'.)

The truth about writing!

If you lack experience in academic writing, it can sometimes feel as if you are a 'novice', 'outside', looking 'in' on the world of 'expert' writers (academics and experienced student writers), where everyone gets everything right first time. But this is far from the truth! In fact, you are a member of a diverse **writing community**, and members across this community, including experienced writers, usually have to work very hard to produce text which is clear and coherent. In order to make sure their writing makes sense to the reader, it is usually necessary for most writers to read and edit their text frequently at all stages of the writing process. It is tempting to believe that you will be able to get away with less editing as you become more experienced in writing, but in fact, research suggests that the more experienced a writer becomes, the more they edit and redraft (Benson and Heidish, 1995). If experienced academics see the value and necessity of the editing and redrafting process, then it seems advisable that you, as a developing academic writer, should follow their example.

Putting yourself in the reader's shoes

If you do not read your own text, you cannot imagine the reader's experience as they navigate the text. You should read your text frequently, *putting yourself in the reader's shoes*. As you read, ask yourself the following questions:

- Would this make sense to someone else?
- Are points and ideas organised according to clear principles?
- Are they in a logical order?
- Are the links between them explicit?
- Is there anything which is vague or ambiguous?
- Does the text *flow*?

When reading and editing, your focus should be on **meaning**; at a later stage, you will need to proofread your text in order to correct surface errors in grammar and punctuation, but this should not be the focus while you are still at the stage of making decisions about content and organisation. You also need to leave time at the end of the writing process to read through the text several times. Again, you should first focus on meaning (before proofreading). Being able to do this also requires good time management: you can't do it if you finish the essay ten minutes before the deadline!

Task

Editing and redrafting for coherence

Look at the following drafts. Text A is accurate and academic in style, but the lecturer reading it found it a little hard to follow, as indicated by the comments. What changes has the writer made in B in order to make the text more coherent for the reader?

What kind of changes?

A

Bit vague — *What?*

Sandford et al (2016) argue that social workers are instrumental in helping service users make <u>changes</u> which could help them improve their long-term mental health prospects <u>because of anxiety</u>. <u>It</u> found that extension of the social work role to hold more anxiety management cases benefited more people without compromising quality of service or outcomes. However, if social workers were to take on an even greater share of working with people with anxiety problems within the inter-disciplinary team, this would have workforce implications.

Not obvious you were discussing social workers <u>working in an inter-disciplinary team</u> up to this point. Do check the way you describe what is happening in the social work role. This could be read

CROSS REFERENCE

Chapter 5, Preparing your work for submission

that social workers are working with people in the team experiencing anxiety problems. I don't think this is what you mean to say.

B

Sandford et al (2016) argue that social workers are instrumental in helping service users with anxiety problems make behavioural changes which could help improve their long term mental health prospects. In their study of interdisciplinary mental health teams, they found no evidence to suggest that extending the social work role to incorporating anxiety management referrals would in any way be detrimental the service provided or outcomes for service users. They did highlight, however, that if social workers were to take on a greater share of anxiety management work, this would have workforce implications that would need to be considered.

CROSS
REFERENCE

Cohesion and
paragraph
structure,
Referring
back in
the text,
Repetition,
variation and
pronoun use

Discussion: editing and redrafting for coherence

Text B is clearer, as it is far more **explicit**.

- The phrase 'behavioural changes' in Text B is much clearer than the rather vague 'changes'.

- Text B is explicit about the study being referred to, and the fact that it is focused on social workers in an inter-disciplinary team. In Text A, the reader only realises that social workers in an inter-disciplinary team are the focus right at the end of the text.

- In Text A, lack of clarity in expression could lead to confusion about who were being supported by the social workers – service users or staff.

- In Text A, the reader is having to guess what 'it' refers to. It is important to be very sure that the reader can trace a pronoun like 'it' or 'they' back to the thing it refers to. This will be discussed later in this chapter.

Writing essay introductions and conclusions

A coherent essay makes things clear for the reader right from the start with a clear **introduction**. The introduction should tell the reader:

- Your purpose in writing. You should refer directly to the essay title or question.

- Some general background information, including the main concepts under discussion, clarifications, definitions etc.

- How you will address the topic in order to achieve your purpose and satisfy the needs and expectations of the reader. You should include a brief overview of what will be included in the essay in order to achieve the stated purpose. The items listed in this overview should reflect the order in which you present them in the essay (and refer to exact subheadings if you have them).

Below is an example introduction for one of the essays referred to earlier in the chapter:

'The core skill of social work is the ability to communicate.' Using appropriate evidence, explore the arguments for and against this proposition.

> It has been claimed that the core skill of social work is communication (Brain, 2014). It is abundantly clear that communication is important in social work practice. Social workers are required to speak to a range of diverse service users and carers and colleagues from across different professions every day. They must also provide written communications, in the form of agency records, for example. However, it could be argued that assessment and intervention skills, intellectual skills, and even general administrative capacity are equally, if not more, important. **The aim of this essay is** to examine the extent to which communication can be considered to be the *core* social work skill. **It will begin by** examining what is meant by the term 'communication' in social work. **It will then** outline what are generally considered to be the core skills required by social workers, with reference to the Professional Capabilities Framework (2012). **It will go on** to examine the impact of communication skills on a range of social work activities, and assess the role that poor communication has played in a number of documented 'failures' in social work practice.

Note the key phrases (in **bold**) used to indicate each section of the essay. Notice also the form of the verb that follows these phrases (the aim is *to do*; begin by *doing*; go on *to do*). These types of phrases, used to guide the reader through a text, are known as **signposts** (discussed later in the chapter). These signposts can be adapted to most essays, and they are a useful tool for ensuring that you have a clear structure. Common verbs for describing what a writer *does* in essays are:

CROSS REFERENCE

Linking ideas

- outline;
- describe;
- identify;
- examine;
- look into;
- analyse;
- evaluate;
- explore.

CROSS REFERENCE

Appendix 3, Key phrases in assignments

These terms are not interchangeable: for example, they can express whether you intend to simply present or describe something, or whether you aim to go deeper. The terms you use should relate to the key terms used in the essay title or question.

Longer essays may have an introduction which provides quite an extended account of the essay context. An example can be seen later in this chapter.

A **conclusion** is the part of the essay where you draw everything together. It usually contains the following:

CROSS REFERENCE

Developing a coherent argument and expressing criticality

- a reference to what was said in the introduction to show that you have achieved your stated purpose;
- a summary of your argument, drawing together the main points discussed in the body of the essay;

- a statement on where you stand on the topic you've discussed, and the significance of this;
- some practical recommendations and/or implications for social work practice.

Below is an example of a conclusion for the same essay.

> In conclusion, good communication skills lie at the heart of all areas of social work practice, and can thus be considered to be at least as important as the assessment, intervention and intellectual skills that a social worker must be proficient in. It is therefore important that communication skills are developed and assessed as part of social work education. However, social workers do not function in isolation. As discussion of a number of reported social work 'failures' in this essay has shown, a breakdown in communication between social workers and other professionals, eg doctors, teachers and health visitors, can result in or contribute to poor practice. Thus, it is clear that effective communication is something which should be prioritised at all levels of practice and effective inter-professional communication should be encouraged and supported.

Cohesion and paragraph structure

A text is made up of paragraphs. For a text to be clear and coherent, each paragraph must have a clear focus and structure. Good paragraphs usually have the following structural characteristics:

- they deal with a single unified point and do not digress from this;
- they often introduce this point in the first sentence;
- they usually move from general to specific information and ideas;
- they order and connect ideas in a logical manner.

In order for a paragraph to develop clearly, the points or ideas it contains should be linked in *meaningful* ways. This meaningful linking is known as 'cohesion' (Halliday and Hassan, 1976), and it is achieved through organisation, grammar and word choice, aspects of which will be discussed in this section. (Note that the extracts in the following task will be referred to throughout this chapter.)

Task

Cohesion and paragraph structure

Read the paragraphs below.

1) Do you find them easy to read?
2) The paragraphs demonstrate some of the typical features of paragraph development and cohesion in English. Can you identify any aspects of organisation, grammar or word choice which make your life easier as a reader?

Extract A: an extract from a typical student essay

One important element of communication in social work is *active listening*, whereby social workers fully concentrate on and reflect on what patients say (Jagger, 2015). According to Mobley (2005), active listening is an effective way of signalling empathy, as it conveys to an individual that they have the full attention of the person they are talking to. One aspect of active listening is verbal communication on the part of the listener, such as restating and summarising the speaker's message (Jagger, 2015). Another important element of active listening is non-verbal communication. It is widely held that words form only a minor percentage of communication (Hargie et al, 2004; Sherman, 1993), and that a large part of any message is conveyed through 'paralanguage', such as tone of voice and intonation, and body language, such as posture, eye contact, facial expressions, gestures and touch (Argyle, 1988). This fact impacts considerably on the active listener, who not only has to be aware of the message conveyed through their own non-verbal communication, but also of any non-verbal clues from the speaker: 'One sigh may be communicating a lifetime of emotions' (Freshwater, 2003, p 93).

Extract B: an extract from a social work textbook (Feldon, 2017, p 252)

It is essential to appreciate that assessments of capacity must always be made in relation to the specific decision to be made. The Mental Capacity Code of Practice 2015 clarifies this as follows:

- a person lacks capacity if 'the impairment or disturbance means that they are unable to make a specific decision at the time it needs to be made' (paragraph 4.3);
- assessment of a person's capacity must not be based on 'their ability to make decisions in general' (paragraph 4.4);
- 'a person may also lack capacity to make a decision about one issue but not about others' (paragraph 4.5);

An illustration of the capacity test is given in paragraph 19.19, which states 'it is not necessary for a person to understand local authority funding arrangements to be able to decide where to live'.

Extract C: an extract from a social work textbook (Cartney, 2011, p 14)

Debates about the interplay between how social workers use formal knowledge, theories and research, and the place of informal knowledge, on-the-job expertise and practice wisdom seem to have been ongoing throughout the history of our profession (Howe, 1992; Payne, 2005). While the relationship between formal knowledge and social work practice is inextricably knitted together, at times the description of this relationship is also characterised by ambivalence, confusion and misunderstandings (Parton, 2000; Sheppard et al, 2000). Earlier debates often distinguished between 'theories of practice' which incorporated explicit theoretical and were usually subject to research-based verification and informal 'practice theories' which drew on the accumulation of practice wisdom and incorporated knowledge generated and used by practitioners which was not usually verified.

Extract D: an (adapted) extract from the discussion section of a research article (Blakemore et al, 2018)

Students need to be encouraged to critically reflect on the interaction between expertise, institutionalised power and personal biases when they give advice to clients or take persuasive action. They need to be encouraged to critique the weight of these elements in relation to client safety, self-determination and autonomy. The study responds to increasing calls to study supportive communication as an interactive process in which the thoughts and behaviours of providers and recipients are mutually influential (McGeorge et al, 2011). Future research should continue to examine the role of advice givers and how advice givers impact advice recipients, and how recipient reactions in turn influence advice giver goals. This is of particular relevance in the professional social work context

General and specific information

As shown in Table 2.1, all the example paragraphs above move from **general** statements to more **specific** information, which is typical of English paragraph structure. General statements at the start of a paragraph often serve to establish the topic of the whole paragraph: these are sometimes called **topic sentences** or **umbrella statements**. As these examples show, specific information can include definitions, explanations, analysis, evidence, evaluation, and exemplification, but this varies depending on the purpose of the writer.

Table 2.1: General and specific content

EXAMPLE TEXT	GENERAL TOPIC	SPECIFIC DETAILS
A	Introduction to and definition of a key concept/term	Relevance, significance, analysis, evidence
B	General statement/claim	Explanation, exemplification
C	General statement/claim	Analysis, evaluation
D	Discussion/ recommendation	Expansion, exemplification, focus on and exemplification of two points (expansion, exemplification and evidence), evidence

Task

General and specific information

Identify and describe the general and specific information in the paragraph below.

> It is important not only to consider your conduct while in work; you must also remember that as a professional and a member of a professional body, you are under scrutiny at all times. Think about when you go out with your friends on a Saturday night. You have a few drinks and let your hair down. Yes that's fine but you MUST consider who may see you, what you are doing and that you are still representing the organisation you work for and your profession ... Unfortunately you are never really off duty in that you are always answerable for your actions.
>
> (Adams and Sheard, 2013, p 24)

Old and new information

To respond to an academic assignment, it is necessary to provide the reader with a lot of information. However, it is also necessary to let the reader know how each new piece of information fits in with what has already been said. The example extracts above demonstrate one typical way of doing this in English: they frequently refer back to **'old'** information given in the previous sentence, or earlier in the text, before supplying **'new'** information. It is a way of staying on topic, linking ideas together, and focusing the reader on the new information. This feature is highlighted below: Extract A repeatedly refers to the main theme of the text (introduced in the first sentence), adding new information each time; the last sentence in A refers back to the theme of the previous sentence.

Theme

One important element of communication in social work is **active listening**, whereby social workers fully concentrate on and reflect on what service users and carers say. According to Mobley (2005), **active listening** is an effective way of signalling empathy, as it conveys to an individual that they have the full attention of the person they are talking to. One aspect of **active listening** is verbal communication on the part of the listener, such as restating and summarising the speaker's message (Jagger, 2015). Another important element of **active listening** is non-verbal communication. It is widely held that words form only a minor percentage of communication (Hargie et al, 2004; Sherman, 1993), and that a large part of any message is conveyed through 'paralanguage', such as tone of voice and intonation, and body language, such as posture, eye contact, facial expressions, gestures and touch (Argyle, 1988). **This fact** impacts considerably on the **active listener**, who not only has to be aware of the message conveyed through their own non-verbal communication, but also of any non-verbal clues from the speaker: 'One sigh may be communicating a lifetime of emotions' (Freshwater, 2003, p 93).

The example below also demonstrates referral back to old information.

> Midwives should be better trained to support women who are diagnosed with HIV. This should include appropriate communication of results, offering individualised support, maintaining confidentiality and providing accurate information on the impact of an HIV positive test. The latter point is particularly important, as some participants automatically believed they had AIDS and that death would be imminent.

Task

Old and new information

 Find the parts of the text below which refer back to information given earlier in the text.

> Patients and service users are being encouraged to take more control of their own care (Department of Health, 2009) and they have an important part to play in determining how services are designed, implemented and evaluated (The Kings Fund, 2012). By collaborating with service users and responding appropriately to their feedback, social workers, nurses and other healthcare staff can deliver more appropriate care and ensure that any concerns raised are dealt with quickly and appropriately (Coulter, 2012). This will usually involve collecting and using information provided by patients (eg patient satisfaction surveys or focus groups) in order to deliver the kind of services that patients want. Whichever approach is used, the key aim is to find out what patients really think about the services we provide and provide supporting evidence of this.
>
> (Adapted from Burns, 2015, p 228)

Referring back in the text: repetition, variation and pronoun use

Reference back to information earlier in the text can be achieved through repetition, as demonstrated in Extract A. Students are sometimes reluctant to repeat as they have been told that repetition will bore the reader or will indicate their lack of knowledge or vocabulary. The truth is that there is good and bad repetition: 'bad' repetition involves the inclusion of redundant information or words, or 'clumsy' reiteration of the same word in sequential sentences; 'good' repetition is a vital part of cohesion (Halliday and Hasan, 1976), and, used carefully, it greatly improves the lucidity of the text for the reader. In Extract A, repetition of the key term reminds the reader what the text is about, and enables them to understand how each new point relates to the central concept in question.

Another way of staying on topic is through 'chains' of related words through a text, for example, the use of words related to 'theory' in the following text.

> Debates about the interplay between how social workers use formal knowledge, **theories** and research, and the place of informal knowledge, on-the-job expertise and practice wisdom seem to have been ongoing throughout the

history of our profession (Howe, 1992; Payne, 2005). While the relationship between **formal knowledge** and social work practice is inextricably knitted together, at times the description of this relationship is also characterised by ambivalence, confusion and misunderstandings (Parton, 2000; Sheppard et al, 2000). Earlier debates often distinguished between **'theories of practice'** which incorporated explicit **theoretical standpoints** and were usually subject to research-based verification and informal **'practice theories'** which drew on the accumulation of practice wisdom and incorporated **knowledge** generated and used by practitioners which was not usually verified.

However, caution should be employed when considering the use of **synonyms** (words which have the same or a similar meaning). You should ask yourself if a synonym really has the same meaning as your original word, particularly if you find it in a thesaurus and haven't used it before. If you are unsure, do not be afraid to repeat the original word. In the case of technical terms (such as 'active listening' in Extract A), you should not usually change these at all ('active hearing' or 'careful listening' are not acceptable because they do not reflect conventional usage in the field).

Sometimes a noun can be referred back to with a pronoun (*it, them, him, her*, etc), eg:

> **Most experienced social workers** take an eclectic approach to using theoretical ideas: **they** have an awareness of the strengths and weaknesses of the various perspectives and models, and **they** use **their** professional judgement to select a theoretical approach most suitable for a given set of circumstances.

When deciding whether to repeat a noun or replace it with a pronoun, ask yourself if the reader will easily understand what the pronoun refers to. If there is any doubt, repeat the noun.

CROSS REFERENCE

Chapter 4, Language in use, Top tips, Using a thesaurus

Task

Noun or pronoun?

Which choice would help the reader most in the text below? (Remember that one choice can affect the following choice, so there are different ways to make the text coherent. The choices you make are about the whole text, not just one sentence.)

> Fatigue is commonly experienced by people suffering from a variety of chronic illnesses. In the sixteenth century, the concept of 1) <u>fatigue/it</u> was related to a tedious duty; nowadays, 2) <u>fatigue/it</u> is understood as a state of feeling tired for 'no reason'; Barsevick et al (2010) define 3) <u>fatigue/it</u> as a subjective state, a feeling unrelated to that of being tired after exercise or relieved after rest. 4) <u>Fatigue/It</u> may be regarded as exhaustive, unpredictable in its course, and affecting cognitive ability. 5) <u>Fatigue/It</u> is often described as multidimensional and

disabling, affecting the quality of life of those living with it. 6) <u>Fatigue/</u>
<u>It</u> is associated with negative emotions such as anxiety, numbness and
vulnerability. These are likely to impact on social relationships and
family life, often leading to withdrawal and social isolation.

(Adapted from Ormrod and Burns, 2015, p 286)

Referring back in the text: useful words and phrases

Here are some examples of particular words and phrases commonly used to refer
back to 'old' information in the previous sentence:

A

Though there are some social workers who rigidly adhere to one or other of
the theoretical frameworks, **these** are the exception rather than the rule.

B

Social workers should be trained in the effective implementation of the Care
Act 2014. **This** should include understanding information from the Act,
regulations and statutory guidance. The **latter point** is particularly important
as the accompanying Care and Support Statutory Guidance (revised 2017) is
not always set out in a way that is coherent from a social work perspective.

(Feldon, 2017, p 1)

C

Nowadays social workers are under pressure to work to support children
being cared for in their families at a time when resources for preventative
work are scarce. In certain circumstances, **this** can lead to additional
pressures on social workers who are striving to do the best jobs they can do
in difficult circumstances.

D

By collaborating with service users and responding appropriately to their
feedback, social workers, nurses and other healthcare staff can deliver more
appropriate care and ensure that any concerns raised are dealt with quickly
and appropriately. **This** will usually involve collecting and using information
provided by patients (eg patient satisfaction surveys or focus groups) in order
to deliver the kind of services that patients want. **Whichever approach** is
used, the key aim is to find out what patients really think about the services
we provide and provide supporting evidence of **this**.

These words and phrases can play a huge role in helping the reader to follow the
development of a text. Common words and phrases used to refer back are: 'this',
'these', 'the' and 'such'. The words 'this' and 'these' can be used alone (as in some of
the examples above), but they (and other words) are often followed by a noun which
repeats or summarises information given in the previous sentence. Drummond (2016)
has identified the most common 'summary nouns' in academic English as:

- time;
- case;
- point;
- view;
- period;

- process;
- approach;
- question;
- problem;
- area.

Following the process for creating similar lists set out in Drummond (2016), the following nouns with specific reference to social work emerge:

- article;
- population
- research;
- sample;
- approach;

- group;
- analysis;
- process;
- type.

These summary nouns have also been called 'signalling nouns' (Flowerdew, 2003), and indeed, writers often choose to refer back to something with a noun which *signals* their own attitude or stance. For example, 'this problem' is subtly different to 'this challenge', the latter possibly signalling a more positive attitude. What's more, the writer might underline their stance by adding an adjective, such as 'serious' or 'minor' before 'problem'. These choices are part of *criticality*, as they convey the writer's interpretation and stance.

CROSS REFERENCE

Developing a coherent argument and expressing criticality

Task

Referring back in the text to summarise and comment

1) In the examples below, link back to the ideas in the first sentence using 'this'/ 'these' and a word from the lists of common summary nouns given earlier in this chapter.

a) Social workers in the local community encouraged volunteers to befriend a group of older people who were isolated after the day centre closed down. This _____ was seen as a way of increasing social contact for older people without relying on council services.

b) Many homeless people receive little or no support from statutory services. Local councils need to rethink their priorities to ensure service provision for this increasing _____.

c) The researchers set out to include a representative sample of people in their study. This _____ enabled the results to be generalised across the broader population.

d) The student analysed the phenomenon in great detail. _____ high level of _____ enabled her to develop a strong argument.

e) Social workers pro-actively engaged the parents in the child's care plan and this _____ reveals the benefits of such an approach.

f) Social workers must research current studies to inform their practice. This _____ allows for an evidenced informed approach to their own practice.

2) How do you think you might refer back to the ideas in the previous sentences to repeat, summarise or comment on an idea?

a) Social workers play an important role in supporting families experiencing difficulties managing. Historically the focus of _____ has been linked to seeking to prevent children entering the care system.

(Kemppainen et al, 2012, p 490)

b) The Lunacy Acts of the mid-nineteenth century essentially created an institutional base for the emerging discipline of psychiatry (Nolan, 1998). Prior to _____, those looking after the mentally ill were often referred to as 'keepers', a somewhat dehumanising term.

(Pryjmachuk, 2011, p 7)

c) If social workers are practising in a professional manner, it is important that they have knowledge of the findings of current research in relation to their area of work. Knowledge of _____ contributes to professional decision making

d) The concept of moral engagement arises from social cognitive theory (Bandura, 1986, 1991) and requires you to stand firm in your moral behaviour, despite the possibility of peer or social pressure to act differently. This takes moral courage. Bandura suggests that a sure way to demonstrate this concept is through empathy. This means you must accept responsibility for your behaviours and demonstrate a humane concern for others at all times. _____ ensures that we are able to consider best practice and best interest for those in our care.

(Lee-Woolf et al, 2015, p 18)

Linking ideas

If the links between ideas are clear and logical, there is often no need to signify them with particular words. In the example below, it is clear that the second sentence explains the reason for the claim in the first sentence.

Another important element of active listening is non-verbal communication. It is widely held that words form only a minor percentage of communication …

Sometimes, **punctuation** alone can be used to signify a link, as in the example below, where a colon is used to signal that what follows is an expansion and explanation.

CROSS REFERENCE

Chapter 4, Language in use, Punctuation and sentence structure, Colons

> Most skilled practitioners take an eclectic approach: they have an awareness of the strengths and weaknesses of the various perspectives and models, and they use their professional judgement to select a treatment approach most suitable for a given set of circumstances.

However, often particular words and phrases can be used to signal the relationship between ideas, as in the examples below.

A

While the individual may not have capacity to make some decisions they may still retain capacity for other decisions. **For example**, a person with a learning disability may lack the the capacity to decide where they live but this does does not necessarily mean that they do not have capacity to decide what to wear, eat and how to spend their time each day.

B

As far as individual social work practice is concerned student social workers learn a great deal from working alongside skilled practice educators. They do need, **however**, to demonstrate that they also have a firm grasp of theoretical and research knowledge to underpin their own interventions.

C

The concept of moral engagement arises from social cognitive theory (Bandura, 1986, 1991) and requires you to stand firm in your moral behaviour, **despite** the possibility of peer or social pressure to act differently.

D

If you are offered a social work student placement in a centre working with users who abuse drugs and/or alcohol, it is very helpful to prepare by finding out about reactions to common drug use before your interview.

E

The fact that social workers engage in preventative and not only safeguarding work can sometimes be overlooked, perhaps **because** of the high profile of the safeguarding functions social workers perform.

F

This will usually involve collecting and using information provided by patients (eg patient satisfaction surveys or focus groups) **in order to** deliver the kind of services that patients want.

G

Though there are some practitioners who rigidly adhere to one or other of the theoretical frameworks, these are the exception rather than the rule.

H

In conclusion, good communication skills lie at the heart of all areas of social work practice, and can **thus** be considered to be at least as important as the assessment and intervention skills that a social worker must be proficient in. It is **therefore** important that communication skills are developed and assessed as part of social work education.

I

In addition to training social workers, support staff (eg receptionists) should **also** be trained to ensure that service users' information remains confidential and breaches of confidentiality do not occur.

These linking words and phrases have very specific functions, as demonstrated in the texts above:

- **addition**: in addition to, also
- **exemplification**: for example
- **purpose**: in order to
- **contrast**: while, however, despite, though
- **reason**: because
- **result**: thus, therefore
- **condition**: given, if

This means they are not easily interchangeable. They should not be used as decoration or to make a text 'sound more academic'. In fact, they should only be introduced into the text when the relationship between ideas is not already clear enough.

Certain linking words and phrases can act as explicit **signposts** for the reader, letting them know, for example, why something is included in the text, or what is coming next.

A

One aspect of active listening is verbal communication on the part of the listener such as restating and summarising the speaker's message (Jagger, 2015). **Another important element of active listening is** body language.

B

The aim of this essay is to examine the extent to which communication can be considered to be the **core** social work skill. **It will begin by** examining what is meant by the term 'communication' in social work. **It will then** outline what are generally considered to be the core skills required by social workers, with reference to the Professional Capabilities Framework (2012). **It will go on** to examine the impact of communication skills on a range of social work activities, and assess the role that poor communication has played in a number of documented 'failures' in social work.

The first example illustrates a structure which is useful for sequencing information and linking new information to a central theme. (Repetition is also important here.) The second example contains typical signposts from essay introductions.

There are clearly many ways to link ideas. The important thing is to make choices based on *meaning*, and the needs of the reader.

Task

Linking ideas

1) Choose the word/phrase which conveys the right meaning in the passages below.

a) Data were collected on the activities of 25 social workers in a hospital setting. <u>In addition/Moreover</u>, interviews were carried out over a three week period.

b) A number of NQSWs reported holding higher caseloads than they felt comfortable with. <u>In contrast/on the contrary</u>, others spoke highly about the suport and protected caseloads they experienced in their first year as a newly qualified practitioner.

c) A number of social workers may be involved with the family, <u>albeit/however</u> at different times.

d) Absorption is the process <u>thereby/whereby</u> a drug passes into the body.

e) The training classes on communicating with young children helped the students <u>hereby/thereby</u> enhancing their communication skills.

f) The report explored the needs of a subgroup of specific service users.

g) It was reported that most service users had attended their weekly and monthly review meetings (64% and 61% <u>respectively/namely</u>).

h) There are now different routes to train as a social worker, either via a university based or an employment based apprenticeship route, with <u>the first/ the former</u> involving a greater proportion of time spent in the universities and the latter/the last involving students being based in their place of work for 80% of their studies.

2) Delete any linking words or phrases which are unnecessary, do not convey the right meaning, or are grammatically incorrect in the following text.

Feelings of anxiety are experienced by everyone at some point in our lives. Furthermore, some people have a specific cause for their anxious feelings, for example if they have divorced, been recently bereaved or moved house. Other people cannot identify a specific trigger for their feelings of anxiety. However, given that when we are anxious everyone experiences similar symptoms, even though they may vary in intensity and frequency. While avoiding situations that make us anxious can provide short term relief, avoidance is not the best long term coping strategy as the anxiety returns when we are represented with the trigger situation.

Developing a coherent argument and expressing criticality

In order to develop a coherent argument, it is necessary to put yourself in the reader's shoes and imagine what the reader will want to know. You must anticipate their questions and guide them carefully through your argument, providing clear signposts so that they don't get lost or stuck. Imagine a very demanding reader!

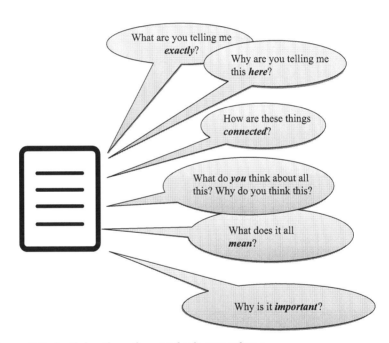

Figure 2.1: Anticipating the reader's questions

Task

Developing a coherent argument

Below is an example of a possible essay title from a social work module:

Discuss the role of family intervention strategies in the treatment of psychosis.

Read the student's discussion of the background to this issue and consider these questions.

1) Do you find the text easy to follow?

2) How has the student made it easy for you? Have they used any of the patterns discussed in this chapter, such as general/specific information, old/new information, referring back in the text, linking and signposts?

3) Have they guided you through their argument and expressed their stance? How?

Research into psychosis has often focused on the role of the family. In the 1950s (when 'schizophrenia' was the more widely adopted term), the focus appeared to be on the family's role in the **causation** of psychosis. Consider, for example, Lidz et al's notion of 'pathological' families (1965) and the 'double-bind' hypothesis of Bateson et al (1956).

Around the same time as these 'causal' hypotheses were being promoted, the anti-psychotic drugs were discovered. Drugs, by their very nature, are treatments designated for the individual, and this fact, coupled with the prevailing view of families as toxic agents led, unsurprisingly, to what could cynically be called the first family intervention strategy – that of excluding the family.

It is at this point that contradictions emerge. Given that the anti-psychotic drugs were so efficacious at attenuating florid psychotic symptoms, many sufferers were able to avoid the long-term hospitalisations that had hitherto accompanied a diagnosis of schizophrenia. Thus, a policy of closure of the large mental hospitals in favour of community care ensued, a policy that implied – even demanded – that families play a role in the care of their relatives. Families, however, continued to receive scant regard from mental health professionals and policy makers. Denied access to support and advice, families were only useful – indeed, it was deemed they had a responsibility – when hospitals were looking to discharge sufferers into the community. As Bebbington and Kuipers remark, relatives were 'often the only people outside the hospital willing to provide continuing care and shelter for the patient' (1982, p 398).

Not surprisingly, this one-sided attitude frustrated and infuriated families and they began to fight back. The inadequacies of community care that became apparent during the 1970s and 1980s, and relatives' feelings that they were overburdened and being saddled with sufferers without support, soon led to the establishment of self-help groups such as the National Schizophrenia Fellowship (now 'Rethink Mental Illness'). The National Schizophrenia Fellowship (1974a, 1974b; Creer and Wing 1988) argued that it was far more productive for mental health professionals to engage, rather than antagonise, relatives and, as the years went by, mental health professionals and successive governments gradually began to listen.

Discussion: developing a coherent argument

Paragraph 1

> **Research into psychosis has often focused on the role of the family**. In the 1950s (when 'schizophrenia' was the more widely adopted term), the focus **appeared to be** on **the family's role** in the *causation* of the disorder. **Consider, for example,** Lidz et al's notion of 'pathological' families (1965) and the 'double-bind' hypothesis of Bateson et al (1956).

The first paragraph immediately references the task ('psychosis', 'the role of the family'), signalling the relevance of the essay content, and identifying supporting literature ('research into psychosis has often focused on'). It then goes on to establish a clear context for the discussion, suggesting that 'the role of the family' may be more complex than anticipated (the writer's caution with regard to this is expressed in the choice of verb – 'appeared to be'); the italics used for 'causation' serve to suggest a contrast with what the reader might expect. The writer refers the reader to examples from scholars as evidence for the pattern he has identified in the literature (focus on the causal role of the family at that time).

Paragraph 2

> Around the same time as **these 'causal' hypotheses** were being promoted, the anti-psychotic **drugs** were discovered. **Drugs, by their very nature**, are treatments designated for the individual, and **this fact, coupled with the prevailing view** of families as toxic agents **led, unsurprisingly**, to what **could cynically be called** the first family intervention strategy – **that of** excluding the family.

The second paragraph begins by referring back to the idea put forward in the first paragraph with 'these' and a **summary noun** ('these 'causal' hypotheses'), then introduces new information (anti-psychotic drugs were discovered at around the same time). This follows the typical **old/new** pattern. The second sentence refers back to this new idea through repetition ('drugs'), and then provides an analysis of how the introduction of these drugs led to the exclusion of the family (again following the **old/new** pattern). The writer signals **cause and effect** ('this fact, coupled with ... led to'), and explanation ('that of'). His addition of the word 'unsurprisingly' suggests he views the stated effect as an inevitable consequence. Other examples of language which signal the writer's interpretation of the facts are 'by their very nature', 'prevailing' and 'could cynically be called'.

Paragraph 3

> **It is at this point that contradictions emerge. Given** that the anti-psychotic drugs were so efficacious at attenuating florid psychotic symptoms, many sufferers were able to avoid the long-term hospitalisations that had hitherto accompanied a diagnosis of schizophrenia. **Thus,** a policy of closure of the large mental hospitals in favour of community care ensued, a policy that implied – even demanded – that families play a role in the care of their relatives. Families, **however,** continued to receive scant regard from mental health professionals and

policy makers. Denied access to support and advice, families were **only** useful – **indeed**, it was deemed they had a responsibility – when hospitals were looking to discharge sufferers into the community. **As Bebbington and Kuipers remark**, relatives were 'often the only people outside the hospital willing to provide continuing care and shelter for the patient' (1982, p 398).

The third paragraph begins with a very explicit **signpost** ('It is at this point that contradictions emerge.'), which clearly signals to the reader that an important stage in the discussion has been reached. Up until this stage, the focus has been on the exclusion of families. This paragraph details how families became important again (but not in a straightforward way, hence the word 'contradictions'). The paragraph then describes a fairly complex set of related factors. It would be easy for the reader to get lost here. However, the writer manages to make everything clear by introducing these factors in a **step-by-step** manner, connecting them through clear chronology and **linking/signposting** language.

1) The patients were able to avoid long-term hospitalisation because of ('given') the drugs.

2) This led to ('thus') the closure of hospitals in favour of community care.

3) But this did not mean ('however') that families were given credit for the new role they were expected to fulfil.

4) In fact, they were undervalued ('*only* useful') and even ('indeed') exploited.

5) Scholars in the literature support this argument ('As Bebbington and Kuipers remark').

Paragraph 4

> **Not surprisingly, this one-sided attitude frustrated** and **infuriated** families and they began to **fight** back. The **inadequacies** of **community care** that became apparent during the 1970s and 1980s, and relatives' feelings that they were **overburdened** and being **saddled with** sufferers without support, soon **led to** the establishment of **self-help** groups such as the National Schizophrenia Fellowship (now 'Rethink Mental Illness'). The National Schizophrenia Fellowship (1974a, 1974b; Creer and Wing 1988) **argued** that it was **far more productive** for mental health professionals to **engage, rather than antagonise**, relatives and, as the years went by, mental health professionals and successive governments gradually began to listen.

This paragraph follows a **general-specific** pattern. The first sentence signals the **problem-solution** organisation of the paragraph, and the rest of the paragraph fleshes this out. There is a clear signal of stance at the beginning of the paragraph 4 ('not surprisingly'). The paragraph then refers back to the idea in the previous paragraph with 'this', a **summary noun**, and an adjective which demonstrates a critical stance ('this *one-sided* attitude'). This again follows the **old/new** pattern. The second sentence also refers back to the concept of 'community care' introduced in the previous paragraph, and then proceeds to describe how attitudes and institutions changed over time. Supporting literature is clearly interpreted with the choice of reporting verb ('argued' suggests that something is evidenced and convincing – compare with 'claimed' or 'suggests'). The **problem-solution** organisation is clearly signalled.

- The problem is introduced at the beginning of the paragraph, underpinned with the use of negative words: 'frustrated', 'infuriated', 'fight', 'inadequacies', 'overburdened', 'saddled with'.
- There is then a key causal verb: 'led to'.
- The solution part of the paragraph is characterised by more positive language: 'self-help', 'far more productive', 'engage'.

CROSS
REFERENCE

Chapter 1,
Academic
writing: text,
process and
criticality,
Writing
critically

The language of criticality

When constructing an argument, writers need to use specific language to express their criticality and their stance (Biber, 2006; Argent, 2017). This includes how certain you are about something, how strongly you feel about something, and the extent to which you are convinced by evidence and the opinions of others. Some examples of this type of language use were mentioned in the previous task, eg:

- the use of language which explicitly conveys opinion ('by their very nature', 'cynically', 'unsurprisingly', 'saddled with');
- the use of **summary nouns** which convey interpretation or opinion regarding what has been previously mentioned ('these causal hypotheses', 'this one-sided attitude');
- the interpretation of supporting literature through the choice of reporting verbs and expressions ('has often focused on', 'the prevailing view', 'remark', 'argued');
- the use of language which conveys degrees of certainty, especially the use of cautious language to avoid overgeneralisation or unsubstantiated claims ('appeared to be', 'could cynically be called').

Task

Identifying stance

Writers have different views depending on the extent of their knowledge and their interpretation of a situation. How do the following sentences differ in the way the writers assess the situation in question?

1a) This drug will limit the side effects of the treatment.

1b) This drug may limit the side effects of the treatment.

2a) Concerns relating to delays in allocating social work cases have been addressed.

2b) Concerns relating to delays in allocating social work cases have to some extent been addressed.

3a) The reason for the decline in teenage pregnancy rates in the UK is improved sex and relationship education.

3b) The principal reason for the reported decline in teenage pregnancy rates in the UK is improved sex and relationship education.

4a) Adult social care in the UK is currently facing numerous serious problems.

4b) Adult social care in the UK is currently facing a number of challenges.

5a) Further research is required on this innovative approach.

5b) Further research is required on this largely untested approach.

6a) Campbell argues that changes in funding will impact poorer communities disproportionately.

6b) Brown claims that changes in funding will impact poorer communities disproportionately.

6c) Darcy et al maintain that changes in funding will impact poorer communities disproportionately.

7a) Li et al advocate the use of a holistic approach to assessment.

7b) Sanders suggests the use of a holistic approach to assessment.

7c) Clark discourages the use of a holistic approach to assessment.

8a) All the community social workers share information.

8b) Crucially, all the community social workers share information.

8c) Worryingly, all the community social workers share information.

Discussion: identifying stance

- In 1), 'will' suggests that the writer has been convinced of the certainty of the 'proposition' (ie the drug does x); 'may' suggests uncertainty on the part of the writer regarding the proposition. The writers are clearly assessing the evidence in different ways.

- In 2), 'to some extent' suggests that the writer believes that many concerns have not yet been addressed.

- In 3), 'principal' suggests that the writer believes there are also other (less important) reasons; the choice of the word 'reported' serves to distance the writer from the claim slightly.

- In 4), 'numerous' means 'many'; 'a number of' means 'some'; the term 'serious problems' suggests a more negative assessment of the situation than 'challenges'.

- In 5), 'innovative' suggests a positive assessment of the situation; 'largely untested' suggests that the writer has concerns.

- In 6), 'argues' suggests that the writer believes Campbell has presented a convincing, well-supported case; 'claims' suggests that the writer sees Brown's view as open to question; 'maintains' suggests that the writer believes Darcy et al are insisting on a view which goes against the majority view or evidence to the contrary.

- In 7), the writers express their interpretation of scholars' views through the choice of verb: 'advocate' means that they strongly recommend something; 'suggest' implies a much weaker recommendation; 'discourage' conveys the opposite of a recommendation.
- In 8), a) is a neutral report of a situation; the addition of the word 'crucially' suggests the writer's belief that this fact is very important or positive; the addition of 'worryingly' suggests the writer's concern about the situation.

Summary

This chapter has looked at the ways in which you can make your writing clear and coherent. It has demonstrated how careful planning and editing can help you to produce a text which a reader can easily navigate and understand. It has shown how to write effective introductions and conclusions, and how to structure clear paragraphs. It has made clear how your choice of language can affect meaning, and impact on the understanding of the reader. It has also demonstrated how arguments can be developed coherently, and expressed through the use of 'critical' language.

Sources of example texts

Adams, J and Sheard, A (2013) *Positive Social Work: The Essential Toolkit for NQSWs*, St. Albans: Critical Publishing.

Blakemore, T, Agllias, K and Pallas, P (2018) 'What You Need to Do Is...' Social Work Students' Reflections on an Advice Giving Audit Exercise. *Journal of Social Work Practice*.

Burns, D (2015) Leadership and Management. In Burns, D (ed) *Foundations of Adult Nursing*. London: Sage, 205–42.

Cartney, P (2011) Consolidating Practice with Children and Families. In Cocker, C and Allain, L (eds) *Advanced Social Work with Children and Families*. London: Sage.

Cornforthe, A (2012) Management of Asthma Care. *Independent Nurse: For Primary Care and Community Nurses* [online]. Available at: www.independentnurse.co.uk/clinical-article/management-of-asthma-care/63632/ (accessed 10 April 2017).

Feldon, P (2017) *The Social Worker's Guide to the Care Act 2014*, St. Albans: Critical Publishing.

Kemppainen, V, Tossavainen, K and Turunen, H (2012) Nurse's Roles in Health Promotion Practice: An Integrative Review. *Health Promotion International*, 28(4), 490–501.

Kendal, S and Pryjmachuk, S (2011) Helping Young People with Mental Health Difficulties. In Pryjmachuk, S (ed) *Mental Health Nursing: An Evidence-Based Introduction*. London: Sage, 331–61.

Lee-Woolf, E, Jones, J, Brooks, J and Timpson, J (2015) Essentials of Nursing: Values, Knowledge, Skills and Practice. In Burns, D (ed) *Foundations of Adult Nursing*. London: Sage, 3–34.

Lingen-Stallard, A, Furber, C and Lavender, T (2016) Testing HIV Positive in Pregnancy: A Phenomenological Study of Women's Experiences. *Midwifery*, 35, 31–8.

Ormrod, J and Burns, D (2015) Supportive Care: Caring for Adults with Long-term Conditions. In Burns, D (ed) *Foundations of Adult Nursing*. London: Sage, 275–312.

Pryjmachuk, S (2011) Theoretical Perspectives in Mental Health Nursing. In Pryjmachuk, S (ed) *Mental Health Nursing: An Evidence-Based Introduction*. London: Sage, 3–41.

References

Argent, S (2017) The Language of Critical Thinking. [online] Available at: www.baleap. org/event/eap-northcritical-thinking (accessed 27 February 2017).

Benson, P and Heidish, P (1995) The ESL Expert: Writing Processes and Classroom Practices. In Belcher, D and Braine, G (eds) *Academic Writing in a Second Language: Essays on Research and Pedagogy*. Norwood, NJ: Ablex, 313–30.

Biber, D (2006) Stance in Spoken and Written University Registers. *Journal of English for Academic Purposes*, 5(2), 97–116.

Drummond, A (2016) An Investigation of Noun Frequencies in Cohesive Nominal Groups. *Journal of Second Language Teaching and Research*, 5(1), 62–88.

Flowerdew, J (2003) Signalling Nouns in Discourse. *English for Specific Purposes*, 22(4), 329–46.

Halliday, M and Hasan, R (1976) *Cohesion in English*. London: Longman.

Jordon, R (2001) *Academic Writing Course: Study Skills in English*. 3rd ed. Harlow: Pearson Education Limited.

Chapter 3
Referring to sources

Learning outcomes

After reading this chapter you will:

- understand the importance of referencing in academic work;

- be aware of different referencing systems;

- be able to apply the Harvard system of referencing in your written work;

- understand how to use sources critically to support your own work and develop your own ideas;

- understand what is meant by the term 'academic malpractice' and learn how to avoid it.

This chapter focuses on referencing, one of the most important academic skills you need to acquire if you are to be successful in your studies. It explains why referencing is so important and how you should go about doing it in your own work. It also discusses how to use sources critically, and how to avoid plagiarism, while illustrating how these two things are often interrelated.

Reflection

1) Why do you think referencing is so important in academic writing?

2) Are you familiar with any particular referencing systems?

3) Have you used any referencing software?

4) What do you think is meant by 'critical' use of sources?

Terminology

The term 'referencing' is generally understood to refer to:

- in-text referencing – the occasions in the main body of a text where you refer to, or quote, the work of others (ie your *sources*);

- the list at the end of the text (usually entitled 'References'), where you list all the sources you have referred to, or quoted, in the text.

In-text references are also sometimes referred to as 'citations', and the verbs 'reference' and 'cite' are both used to refer to the practice of referring to sources.

Why should I reference?

Accurate referencing of academic work is essential for the following reasons.

- It is a form of academic 'courtesy', both to the writer (by acknowledging their work) and to the reader (by helping them to find the source easily).

- It indicates that you have consulted authorities and checked your facts, allowing the reader to have confidence in what you write.

- It signals that you have contextualised your ideas in a wider framework, linking your work to work done previously by other scholars.

- It shows the reader that you have used the literature to build your own ideas.

- It signals that your ideas are founded upon scholarship, and thus have credibility.

- It signals you, as a writer, are situated within the social work knowledge community.

- It shows that you are not pretending to be the source of information or ideas found in sources, ie that you are not attempting to **plagiarise**.

CROSS REFERENCE

Studying for your Social Work Degree, Chapter 3, Becoming a member of your academic and professional community

How should I reference?

There are two main referencing systems, each named after the universities where they originated:

- The **Harvard** system, sometimes referred to as the 'name-date' or 'author-date' system;

- The **Vancouver** system, sometimes referred to as the 'number' or 'citation-sequence' system.

Both systems are used in health and social care disciplines, and examples of both will be given in this chapter. However, the most commonly used system in social work degrees is the Harvard system, so this will be analysed in more detail.

CROSS REFERENCE

Using sources critically

The Harvard system

In this system, sources are identified in the main body of the text according to the surname(s) of the author(s) and the publication year of the source, usually separated by a comma. At the end of the text, all references mentioned in the text are presented in **alphabetical order**, according to author surname (or the surname of the first author when there are multiple authors). Note that the reference forms part of the clause or sentence, so comes before any punctuation.

Example (main text)

Debates about the interplay between how social workers use formal knowledge, theories and research, and the place of informal knowledge, on-the-job expertise and practice wisdom seem to have been ongoing throughout the history of our profession (Howe, 1992; Payne, 2005). While the relationship between formal knowledge and social work practice is inextricably knitted together, at times the description of this relationship is also characterised by ambivalence, confusion and misunderstandings (Parton, 2000; Sheppard et al, 2000).

Example (final reference list)

Howe, D (1992) *An Introduction to Social Work Theory*. Aldershot: Arena.

Parton, N (2000) Some Thoughts on the Relationship between Theory and Practice in and for Social Work. *British Journal of Social Work*, 30, 449–63.

Payne, M (2005) *Modern Social Work Theory* (3rd edition). Basingstoke: Palgrave Macmillan.

Sheppard, M, Newstead, S, Di Caccavo, A and Ryan, K (2000) Reflexivity and the Development of Process Knowledge in Social Work: A Classification and Empirical Study. *British Journal of Social Work*, 30, 465–88.

The Vancouver system

In this system, sources are numbered in the text. The first piece of work you cite becomes reference number 1, the second reference number 2, and so on. At the end of the text, all references mentioned in the text are presented in **numerical order**. Each source only has one number. Thus, if you mention source 1 again later in the text, it retains its number 1, and this is its only number in the final list. Note that the reference forms part of the clause or sentence, so comes before any punctuation.

Example (main body)

Debates about the interplay between how social workers use formal knowledge, theories and research, and the place of informal knowledge, on-the-job expertise and practice wisdom seem to have been ongoing throughout the history of our profession[1,2]. While the relationship between formal knowledge and social work practice is inextricably knitted together, at times the description of this relationship is also characterised by ambivalence, confusion and misunderstandings[3,4].

Example (final list)

1) Howe, D (1992) *An Introduction to Social Work Theory*. Aldershot, Arena.

2) Payne, M (2005) *Modern Social Work Theory*. Basingstoke, Palgrave Macmillan.

3) Parton, N (2000) Some thoughts on the relationship between theory and practice in and for social work. *British Journal of Social Work*, 30, 449–63.

4) Sheppard, M, Newstead, S, Di Caccavo, A and Ryan, K (2000) Reflexivity and the Development of Process Knowledge in Social Work: A Classification and Empirical Study. *British Journal of Social Work*, 30, 465–88.

Referencing styles

Few health and social care publications use the Vancouver system, although some very prestigious ones do, eg the *British Medical Journal*. The Harvard system is much more common in health and social care, and is used in the *British Journal of Social Work*, the *Journal of Social Work Practice* and the *Journal of Advanced Nursing*, for example.

Within the Harvard and Vancouver systems, there are slight variations between publishers. Each publisher has a particular style – sometimes called a 'house style' – of referencing, ie how they want references presented in their books, journals, etc. This will be a version of either the Harvard or Vancouver systems, with their own particular specifications regarding, for example, the way names are given or the use of commas. This book uses the Harvard system, and examples of Harvard referencing are given in the house style of the book's publisher, Critical Publishing.

A well-known example of a particular style in healthcare disciplines is APA, the style of the American Psychological Association. Your university and your specific department will almost certainly have their own styles: they may adopt a style such as APA, or they may devise their own style. It is essential to know which style is required in a particular assignment. Once you are sure of the requirements, the important thing is to provide references which are **complete**, **accurate** and **consistent**. Some common style variations will be mentioned in the following sections.

Using the Harvard system

In social work, you will probably be required to use the Harvard system. This section provides general guidelines.

In-text conventions in the Harvard system

In terms of in-text usage, the Harvard system is slightly more complicated than the number system, and there are some conventions that you should be aware of.

Multiple references

When listing multiple sources in the main body of text, it is usually the convention to list them chronologically, with publications from the same year listed alphabetically; they are usually separated with semi-colons, eg:

(Li, 2002; James and Roberts, 2007; Jones; 2007)

If an author has published two works in the same year, the year is followed by a, b etc (explained in more detail later in the chapter), eg:

(Li, 2002b)

CROSS REFERENCE

Compiling your list of references

Direct quotations

Quotations should be used judiciously. Overuse of quotation can be a symptom of an uncritical 'patchwork' use of references, or even plagiarism. You should only quote something if it is particularly interesting or powerful, and it is not always necessary, or most effective, to quote whole sentences. (See example below.)

CROSS REFERENCE

Critical use of sources

In your text:

- Direct quotations are usually enclosed in 'single' or "double" inverted commas. Follow any guidelines provided on this by your lecturers and be consistent throughout the text.
- A full sentence quotation is introduced with a colon; quoted words or phrases are integrated into your own sentences.
- Page numbers must be provided as part of the reference.
- A quotation must be copied *exactly* as it is written in the book or article from which it has been taken.
- Any words missed out must be indicated by the use of an ellipsis (three dots …). (Sometimes these are enclosed in square brackets to indicate that the omission is yours and not the original author's.)
- Any words inserted or changed (to make the quotation fit in with your own grammar and meaning) must be enclosed in square brackets.
- Long quotations require double indenting and/or a smaller typeface.

Examples

Longer quote

According to Richie and Lewis (2003, p 185):

> A good focus group is more than the sum of its parts. The researcher harnesses the group process, encouraging the group to work together to generate more in-depth data based on interaction […]. [He or she] helps the group create a reflective environment in which the group can take an issue, approach it as they choose and explore it fully.

Shorter quotes

Richie and Lewis (2003) see a good focus group as 'more than the sum of its parts' (p 185). The researcher facilitates the group dynamic, leading to the generation of 'more in-depth data based on interaction' (p 185).

The use of 'et al'

The Latin phrase 'et al' means 'and others'. In health and social care, it is not uncommon to find articles written by as many as five or more authors. In such circumstances, in-text referencing can get a bit messy, so the format 'first-author et al' is used whenever there are three or more authors.

Note that in the final reference list, you must list *all* of the authors regardless of how many authors there are, unless a house style demands otherwise.

Compiling your final list of references in the Harvard system

The final reference list appears at the end of an assignment, paper or publication, in alphabetical order in the Harvard system. It is usual to precede the list with the simple heading 'References'. This term implies a **one-to-one match** between in-text references and the sources included in the final reference list, ie if a source is in the reference list, it should have been cited in the main body of text and any citation in the main body of text should be listed in the final reference list. The term 'bibliography' is sometimes used in books; it has the wider sense of 'sources of information on this subject' which generally inform a piece of work; this approach is not suitable in an academic assignment, so the term 'references', with its more restricted meaning, is usually required.

There are essentially three main types of hard copy publication you will come across:

- books;
- chapters in edited books;
- journal articles.

In this section, guidelines will be provided on how to reference these and other types of reference. Examples will follow the house style of Critical Publishing, but remember that styles vary, and you will need to find out what is required in your department.

Referencing books

There are two types of book that you will encounter: **standard textbooks**, where the authors have written the entire textbook from beginning to end, and **edited textbooks**, where many different authors have written individual chapters which are subsequently collated by an editor or group of editors. The general format for referencing textbooks is:

Surname[s] of author[s], Initial[s] (Year) *Title: Subtitle*. Edition [if 2nd or greater]. Place of publication: Publisher.

Examples

Ferguson, I and Woodward, R (2009) *Radical Social Work in Practice*. Bristol: Policy Press.

Gross, R (2015) *Psychology: The Science of Mind and Behaviour*. 7th ed. London: Hodder Education.

Musson, P (2017) *Making Sense of Theory and its Application to Social Work Practice*. St Albans: Critical Publishing.

When referring to an edited textbook in its entirety, the abbreviation 'ed' (editor) or 'eds' (editors) is inserted before the publication year.

Examples

Hingley-Jones, H, Parkinson, C and Allain, A (eds) (2017) *Observation in Health and Social Care: Applications for Learning, Research and Practice with Children and Adults*. London: Jessica Kingsley.

Lishman, J, Yuill, C, Brannan, J and Gibson, A (2014) *Social Work: An Introduction*. London: Sage.

Referencing chapters in edited books

It is important to distinguish between a straightforward textbook and an edited textbook when referencing. With edited books, different people write the individual chapters and each chapter is treated as a separate article. This means that if students read and make reference to, say, four chapters in an edited book with ten chapters, four references will need to be added to the reference list. The general format for chapters in edited textbooks is:

Surname[s] of chapter author[s], Initial[s] (Year) Title of Chapter. In Surname[s] of editor[s] of book, Initial[s] (ed[s]) *Title of Book: Subtitle of Book*. Edition [if 2nd or greater]. Place of publication: Publisher.

Examples

Briggs, S (2017) Working with Troubled Adolescents: Observation as a Key Skill for Practitioners. In Hingley-Jones, H, Parkinson, C and Allain, A (eds) *Observation in Health and Social Care: Applications for Learning, Research and Practice with Children and Adults*. London: Jessica Kingsley.

Mitchell, K M, Bozarth, J D and Krauft, C C (1977) A Reappraisal of the Therapeutic Effectiveness of Accurate Empathy, Nonpossessive Warmth, and Genuineness. In Gurman, A S and Razin, A M (eds) *Effective Psychotherapy: A Handbook of Research*. Oxford: Pergamon.

Schön, D A (1988) From Technical Rationality to Reflection-in-Action. In Dowie, J and Elstein, A (eds) *Professional Judgement: A Reader in Clinical Decision Making*. Cambridge: Cambridge University Press.

Referencing journal articles

The general format for journal articles is:

Surname[s] of author[s], Initial[s] (Year) Title of Article. *Journal Title*, Volume(Part), Pages.

Examples

Asbury, J (1995) Overview of Focus Group Research. *Qualitative Health Research*, 5(4), 414–20.

Friars, P and Mellor, D (2009) Drop-Out from Parenting Training Programmes: A Retrospective Study. *Journal of Child and Adolescent Mental Health*, 21(1), 29–38.

Rustin, M (2014) The Relevance of Infant Observation for Early Intervention: Containment in Theory and Practice. *Infant Observation*, 17(2), 97–114.

Since PDF copies of journal articles are identical to their print counterparts, it is acceptable to reference electronically accessed versions as the print counterpart, since this will provide sufficient information for a reader (or marker) to locate the resource if required.

In addition, the use of the 'digital object identifier' (DOI) – which is a permanent address for documents on the internet – is likely to become more prevalent in the future. Thus, all of the following variants for referencing journal articles are acceptable in student work:

Friars, P and Mellor, D (2009) Drop-Out from Parenting Training Programmes: A Retrospective Study. *Journal of Child and Adolescent Mental Health*, 21(1), 29–38.

Friars, P and Mellor, D (2009) Drop-Out from Parenting Training Programmes: A Retrospective Study. *Journal of Child and Adolescent Mental Health*, 21(1), 29–38. Available at: www.tandfonline.com/doi/pdf/10.2989/ JCAMH.2009.21.1.5.807 (accessed 7 January 2015).

Friars, P and Mellor, D (2009) Drop-Out from Parenting Training Programmes: A Retrospective Study. *Journal of Child and Adolescent Mental Health*, 21(1), 29–38. DOI:10.2989/JCAMH.2009.21.1.5.807

Theses and dissertations

Theses and dissertations (for example, PhD and MSc theses) follow a format that is very similar to books, except following the title, [type of thesis], [location of university: name of university] appears, for example:

Smith, H (2017) *Relationship Building in Statutory Social Work: A Qualitative Study.* Unpublished thesis. Leicester: De Montfort University.

Conference proceedings

Conference proceedings are printed documents reflecting the content of a conference. They are dealt with in the same way as chapters in edited textbooks.

Example

Cappanera, P, Scutellà, M G and Visintin, F (2014) Home Care Service Delivery: Equity versus Efficiency in Optimization Models. In Matta, A, Li, J, Sahin, E, Lanzarone, E and Fowler, J (eds) *Proceedings of the International Conference on Health Care Systems Engineering.* New York, NY: Springer.

Newspapers and magazines

Occasionally, you might need to reference an article in a newspaper or magazine, but bear in mind the quality of the newspaper or magazine being used. The format for newspapers and magazines is much the same as for journal articles, except that the full date of the issue is required.

Example

Marks, N (2014) Guardian Readers Reveal what Makes them Happy at Work. *The Guardian*, 11 June [online]. Available at: www.theguardian.com/sustainable- business/happy-work-what-makes-you www.theguardian.com/sustainable-business/ happy-work-what-makes-you (accessed 25 October 2016).

Organisational or 'corporate' authors

Institutions and organisations produce many papers and documents. These often cause referencing problems. Remember, however, that these institutions and organisations can be authors in their own right and thus it is fairly easy to reference material by these bodies as the name you need for a name-year system is simply the organisation's name.

So, the Department of Health, the Department for Education, and the Health and Care Professions Council can all be cited as authors – Department of Health

(2008), Department for Education (2014), Health and Care Professions Council (2012), for example.

Examples

Department of Health (2016) *Department of Health Strategic Statement for Social Work with Adults in England 2016–2020*. London: Department of Health.

Department for Education (2015) *Knowledge and Skills Statement for Child and Family Social Workers*. London: TSO.

Health and Care Professions Council (2017) *Standards of Proficiency: Social Workers in England*. London: HCPC.

Common problems in referencing

'Anonymous' authors

With some documents, such as dictionaries or Acts of Parliament, it is difficult to find out who the author is. In these cases, it is acceptable to reference by the document or series title.

Examples

Collins English Dictionary (2011) 11th ed. Glasgow: William Collins & Sons.

Mental Capacity Act (2005) London: HMSO.

Authors with multiple outputs in the same year

Some authors produce several publications in one year. If two or more articles are attributed to the same author or group of authors in a particular year, you need to use some means of distinguishing between the articles. For example, if you use three papers written by Dianne Jones and published in 2004 in an assignment, how would a reader know which paper 'Jones (2004)' refers to? It could be any of the three. (This isn't a problem with Vancouver-style approaches as you would give each paper a separate number as you used it.)

The way to do this in the Harvard system is to use alphabetical sequencing (a, b, c, etc) to distinguish between the articles. So you call the first paper you use Jones (2004a), the second, Jones (2004b), the third, Jones (2004c). The references in the final list would therefore be:

Jones, D (2004a) [Title, etc of first Jones paper you cite.]

Jones, D (2004b) [Title, etc of second Jones paper you cite.]

Jones, D (2004c) [Title, etc of third Jones paper you cite.]

Note that *you*, as the writer, have inserted the letters a, b, c after the publication year. They are not fixed like the publication year, but serve only to distinguish between the three 2004 Jones articles you are using. If you only used one of the Jones papers, you would not need to use any letters after the publication year.

Secondary citations

Sometimes, students make use of references they find in books and articles they have been reading, but do not actually consult the original sources. To present these secondary references as primary references is really a form of academic malpractice. To avoid this, you should ideally follow up the secondary references and consult the original sources. Where this is genuinely not possible, you can make use of the phrases 'cited in' or 'cited by' to acknowledge that the reference is a secondary reference. Secondary references are usually presented as follows:

In the text:

(Parry, 2003, cited in Cartney and Rouse, 2006).

In the list of references:

Cartney, P and Rouse, A (2006) The Emotional Impact of Learning in Small Groups: Highlighting the Impact on Student Progression and Retention. *Teaching in Higher Education*, 11(1), 79–91.

Electronic sources of information

Increasingly, students are making use of electronic sources of information such as the Internet, e-journals and PDF documents when undertaking assignments. Providing that the information employed is in a legitimate format and from a legitimate source (eg a reputable organisation), such information can be extremely valuable. For in-text referencing, the format for electronic sources of information is very much the same as for hard copy material, ie you need a name and a publication year. For compiling the final reference list, the format for referencing electronic material is similar to the format for books and journal articles, except that some additional information is required:

- The type of medium – webpage, PDF, DVD, computer program, etc. – is required (in square brackets) after the resource/document details.

- Following the type of medium, use the phrase 'Available at' or 'Available from' followed by information about the source of the material used, eg the specific computer program, web page, etc.

- The access date (in brackets) is required after the source.

- If no creation/publication date is available for the electronic material, simply write 'no date' where the publication year would normally go.

- If no author can be found, follow the guidance given above for anonymous authors.

Examples

Merriam-Webster Dictionary. [online] Available at: www.merriam-webster.com (accessed 15 May 2017).

Health and Care Professions Council (2017) *Continuing Professional Development and Your Registration*. [online] Available at: www.hcpc-uk.org/publications/index. asp?id=103#publicationSearchResults (accessed 23 March 2018).

There is still debate about how to reference electronic material correctly so don't worry too much about any minor differences in approaches that you come across.

Variations in referencing

Although referencing systems are dependent on some set rules, there is a degree of flexibility, mainly brought about by differences in the house styles of various publishers and organisations. The important thing is to follow guidelines and to make sure that your references are complete, accurate and consistent – don't mix and match in the same piece of work. The following variations are common in the Harvard system:

In-text

- A comma is usual between the name and date, but is sometimes omitted, eg (Thomas 2016) rather than (Thomas, 2016).
- Page numbers for direct quotes can be either preceded by a comma and 'p' or 'p.' ('pp' or 'pp.' for a page range), or by a colon, eg (Thomas, 2016, p. 36) or (Thomas, 2016: 36).
- The phrase 'et al' is sometimes written 'et al.' or '*et al.*'.

Final list

- For journal articles, **bold** is often used to indicate volumes, eg:

  Friars, P and Mellor, D (2009) Drop-Out from Parenting Training Programmes: A Retrospective Study. *Journal of Child and Adolescent Mental Health*, **21**(1), 29–38.

- Page numbers are sometimes preceded by p/pp or p./pp.
- Initials are often followed with full stops to indicate the abbreviation, eg:

  Cocker, C and Allain, L (eds) (2011) *Advanced Social Work with Children and Families*. London: Learning Matters.

- Full first names are sometimes used instead of initials, eg:

  Cocker, Christine and Allain, Lucille (eds) (2011) *Advanced Social Work with Children and Families*. London: Learning Matters.

- The abbreviations 'ed' and 'eds' are often followed by full stops – 'ed.', 'eds.'
- Titles can be in lower case (apart from the first word and proper nouns), or they can be capitalised throughout (apart from 'grammar' words such as prepositions and pronouns), or they can distinguish between titles and subtitles, eg:

  Swales, J and Feak, C (2012) *Academic writing for graduate students: essential tasks and skills*. 3rd ed. Michigan: Michigan ELT.

Swales, J and Feak, C (2012) *Academic Writing for Graduate Students: Essential Tasks and Skills*. 3rd ed. Michigan: Michigan ELT.

Swales, J and Feak, C (2012) *Academic Writing for Graduate Students: Essential tasks and skills*. 3rd ed. Michigan: Michigan ELT.

Task

Referencing errors

1) Below are a number of entries than might appear in a text. What problems can you identify and correct?

   a) According to Tarrier and Barrowclough, carers need information, and professionals have a moral duty to supply it.

   b) The major hindrance appears to be the cultural dominance of 'technical rationality'. Schön 1988.

   c) In a theoretical paper, Dickoff and James (1968) argue this position, which is subsequently backed up by a further, data-based paper (Dickoff and James 1968).

   d) Meleis [2001] speculates that historical and cultural paternalism are largely to blame.

   e) When looking at how professionals develop their expertise, Benner 1984 states that expertise develops when the clinician tests and refines propositions, hypotheses and principle-based expectations in actual practice situations.

   f) According to Green, H (2016) women are the primary carers in society.

   g) The results are consistent with the findings of Posner, Wilson and Kraj (2012).

   h) Smith [cited by Jones 2014] suggests that the findings are incomplete.

   i) … (see, for example, Lewin's 'change spiral' in his book of 1958).

   j) (Schön 1988) suggests that this paradox can be resolved by acknowledging the importance of subjectivity.

2) Below are a number of entries than might appear in a final reference list. What problems can you identify and correct?

   a) Koprowska, J. (2014) *Communication and Interpersonal Skills in Social Work*. Exeter: Learning Matters.

   b) Lloyd, C., King, R., and Chenoweth, L. (2002) *Social Work, Stress and Burnout: A Review*. Journal of Mental Health, 11(3), 255–65.

   c) Payne, M. (2014) Modern Social Work Theory. London: Palgrave Macmilla.

   d) Matthias, M S et al (2012) Decision Making in Recovery-oriented Mental Health Care. *Psych Rehab Journal*, 35, 305–14.

   e) Judd, R G and Johnston, L B (2012) Ethical Consequences of Using Social Network Sites for Students in Professional Social Work Programs. Journal of Social Work Values and Ethics.

f) Kinman and Grant (2011) *Exploring Stress Resilience in Trainee Social Workers: The Role of Emotional Intelligence and Social Competencies.* BJSW, 41.

g) Reducing re-offending by ex-prisoners. Social Exclusion Unit, London (2002).

h) Parsonage et al (2012) https://www.centreformentalhealth.org.uk/liaison-psychiatry-nhs [accessed 14 May].

Top tips

Referencing software

There are a number of referencing software packages that you may choose to use, eg **Endnote**, **Mendeley**, **Zotero** and **Papyrus**, but this is a purely personal decision. They have advantages: they ensure that there is always a one-to-one match between your in-text references and those listed in the final reference list; you can switch automatically and painlessly between different house styles (even between Harvard and Vancouver). They also have disadvantages: you may not be able to get the software on your home computer without buying it (and it can be quite expensive); and their integration into word processing packages can be problematic, causing formatting glitches, for example.

Using sources critically

It is important to know the rules for referencing, but this is just part of the bigger picture. Many students feel confused about referencing. Look at the typical comments below. Do you ever feel like this?

Case studies

1) 'I worry about using too many references. I think it won't be my ideas in the essay.'

2) 'I found a lot of good quotes for my essay, but the lecturer said that it was too descriptive and that I didn't have an argument.'

3) 'I spent ages paraphrasing – changing every word of the original text so that I don't plagiarise and get into trouble. But the lecturer didn't think I had understood the ideas in the literature. She also said my language was "awkward".'

4) 'I found lots of opinions on this subject but I don't know how to make them into an essay.'

5) 'The lecturer said I should give my own opinion, but I'm worried that I'm not as expert as the people writing in books and journals.'

These concerns are understandable. Using sources critically is one of the biggest challenges of university study, and well-meaning advice can often appear contradictory. Firstly, it is important to understand that using references is not a negative thing. On the contrary, it is a positive thing, as it shows you have researched the topic. However, in order for references to enhance your work, they must be used *critically*. Table 3.1 illustrates exactly what this means.

Table 3.1: Critical use of sources

UNCRITICAL USE OF SOURCES	CRITICAL USE OF SOURCES
Other voices dominate your essay.	References to other scholars support your voice, but don't replace it.
You mostly *describe* the contents of the literature; you mostly engage in 'knowledge-*telling*' (Beirerter and Scardamalia, 1987).	You describe, *analyse* and *evaluate* the contents of the literature; you engage in 'knowledge-*transforming*', ie *doing* something purposeful with knowledge (Beirerter and Scardamalia, 1987).
You use paraphrasing to report what scholars say, staying quite close to the original text and replacing individual words with synonyms (to avoid plagiarism).	You demonstrate understanding by paraphrasing in your own words. You try to convey the sense of the sources you refer to, or to interpret them, in a way that supports your argument and acts as a springboard for your own ideas.
There is an over-reliance on quotation. You build your essay around impressive quotations which you think speak for themselves.	You *explain* quotations and integrate them into your own argument; you use quotations to build, support and underline arguments.
You provide a 'patchwork' of references, merely reporting what each individual says, without considering how sources relate to each other or to your argument.	Sources are grouped according to common threads, or compared and contrasted.
You present sources in a random order.	You identify developments, patterns and relationships in the literature, and this determines their place in your essay.
You expect the reader to make the connection between the literature and the context of the assignment.	You explicitly relate what you find in the literature to the context of the assignment; you establish a clear link between your work and the work previously done by other scholars, showing how it has helped you build your ideas.

Advanced skills

Originality

The concept of originality is often misunderstood. It does not mean that you spontaneously make up your own theory or come up with a brand new idea. It means treating the topic in question in a way that is *unique* to *you*, perhaps finding a new way of looking at something. This usually entails appraising viewpoints and evidence on a specific topic or issue, and coming up with your own ideas about it based on what you have been convinced by. To be credible, academic work should be grounded in the literature of your discipline, as knowledge can only really advance – in your mind or in the discipline as a whole – if it is based on and builds on what has gone before. So the work and ideas of other scholars should of course feature heavily in your work. However, the strongest voice in your work should always be your own. If you can approach what you read and hear critically, and use the ideas of others not only to explore an area of knowledge, but also to inform and shape your own argument, you will be making an original contribution to the subject.

Task

Critical use of sources

Which texts best demonstrate critical use of sources? How?

A

Kessler et al (2005) state that mental health problems in the general population frequently commence in adolescence. School-based services for early identification and intervention and for care coordination in primary care are advocated in the USA (Taras, 2004) and many other European countries (Braddick et al, 2009).

B

As mental health problems in the general population frequently commence in adolescence (Kessler et al, 2005), there is a strong case for embedding the skills of recognition and basic management into wider health and education services. Indeed, school-based services for early identification and intervention and for care coordination in primary care are advocated in the USA (Taras, 2004) and in many other European countries (Braddick et al, 2009).

C

While poor access to health-related information in signed languages has been identified as a significant component of health inequalities for Deaf communities around the world (Sign Health, 2009; Graybill et al, 2010; Alexander et al 2012; Fellinger et al 2012; Rogers et al 2013; Sign Health, 2014) there has been little attention to dementia in this respect. Some information on dementia has been produced in BSL on DVD (Scottish Intercollegiate Guidelines Network, 2007; Deaf Connections, 2008), but no evaluation has been carried out of whether the media of its distribution is effective nor whether it has resulted in increased awareness and understanding.

(taken from Young et al, 2016, p 40)

D

There have been a number of studies identifying poor access to health-related information in signed languages as a significant component of health inequalities (Sign Health, 2009; Graybill et al, 2010; Alexander et al, 2012; Fellinger et al, 2012; Rogers et al, 2013; Sign Health, 2014). Furthermore, some information on dementia has been produced in BSL on DVD (Scottish Intercollegiate Guidelines, 2018).

E

Cotgrove (2007) questions the effectiveness of psychological therapies for young people with depression such as CBT and family therapy, and claims that antidepressants have better outcomes. Timini (2007) believes that most childhood distress is self-limiting and does not require extensive intervention. He questions the effectiveness of antidepressants, claiming that scientific accuracy is being sacrificed to marketing spin, and that there may be a link between antidepressants and suicide.

F

There is some debate regarding the use of antidepressants to treat young people. On the one hand, Cotgrove (2007) points to evidence showing the benefits of treatment with antidepressants. He suggests that these treatments are more effective than psychological therapies for young people with depression such as CBT and family therapy. In contrast, Timini (2007) questions the effectiveness of antidepressants, claiming that scientific accuracy is being sacrificed to marketing spin, and even going so far as to suggest a link between antidepressants and suicide. In fact, he questions whether intervention is always necessary, believing that most childhood distress is by nature self-limiting.

Discussion: critical use of sources

Texts A, D and E simply repeat what the literature says – the writer's voice is not apparent; text B (Pryjmachuk et al, 2011) uses the literature to support an argument ('As … there is a strong case for … Indeed …'). Text C from Young et al, 2016, p 40) critiques the use of the sources used rather than simply describing what the research studies say. They identify gaps in knowledge and where more in-depth evaluation would be helpful. Text F (student writing) identifies a clear contrast ('on the one hand', 'in contrast'), and the writer's voice is clearly driving the text ('There is some debate', 'even going so far as', 'in fact').

One simple aspect of criticality in source use is the focus that the writer affords information. One of the ways this expresses itself is in the use of

author-prominent or **information-prominent** sentences. When a writer uses an author-prominent sentence, they place some degree of importance on *who* has written something, as well as what they have written, and the author's name forms part of the sentence structure, eg:

In contrast, Timini (2007) questions the effectiveness of antidepressants

When a writer uses an information-prominent sentence, they focus primarily on *what* is being said, and the author's name is only mentioned in the reference, eg:

As mental health problems in the general population frequently commence in adolescence (Kessler et al, 2005)

In texts B and C, there is a clear focus on information, reflected in the information-prominent sentences. In F (and even E), there is a focus on key players in an important debate. Texts A and D use a mixture of information- and author-focused sentences, but their use appears to be quite random.

Task

Focus

1) Identify which of the sentences below are:

- author-prominent;
- information prominent.

2) In author prominent sentences, a writer can convey their view of a scholar's ideas with the verbs or expressions they choose to use to report them. Which verbs and expressions are used in the author-prominent examples?

a) As Wright (1993) points out, one of the paradoxes of successful change is that it escapes public notice simply because it is successful.

b) One of the paradoxes of successful change is that it escapes public notice simply because it is successful (Wright, 1993).

c) According to Scheidlinger and Aronson (2001), group therapy has been used to treat a wide range of symptomolotalogy in adolescents.

d) Group therapy has been used to treat a wide range of symptomolotalogy in adolescents (Scheidlinger and Aronson, 2001).

e) Musson (2017) argues that psychodynamic theory can offer important insights to guide social work assessment and analysis.

f) Psychodynamic theory can offer important insights to guide social work assessment and analysis (Musson, 2017).

3) Listed below are some verbs commonly used by writers to convey their understanding and interpretation of the literature.

acknowledge; advocate; argue that; identify; define something as; distinguish between

Below are some social work texts, followed by a student's paraphrase. Choose the best verb from the list above to complete each paraphrase so that it conveys the sense of the original text.

A

Text

Students need to be encouraged to critically reflect on the interaction between expertise, institutionalised power and personal biases when they give advice to clients or take persuasive action.

(Blackmore et al, 2018)

Paraphrase

Blackmore et al (2018) _____ encouraging students to critically reflect on the process of advice giving.

B

Text

Following data analysis, four principal themes emerged from the data, each containing several subthemes.

(Pryjmachuk et al, 2011, p 852)

Paraphrase

Pryjmachuk et al (2011) _____ four principle themes.

C

Text

Like most qualitative findings, elements may only be transferrable to similar contexts.

(Lingen-Stallard et al, 2016, p 37)

Paraphrase

Lingen-Stallard et al (2016) _____ the limitations of the study.

D

Text

Postnatal depression may be mild or severe. While milder forms might be treated within the primary healthcare team, more severe forms will need additional input from psychiatric services.

(Adapted from Taylor, 2015, p 145)

Paraphrase

Taylor (2015) _____ mild and severe forms of postnatal depression.

E

Text

Applying behaviourist theory to social work practice predominantly deals with the 'present' addressing *presenting behaviours.*

(Musson, 2017, p 49)

Paraphrase

Musson _____ social workers use behaviourist ideas in their work to focus on the 'present' (2018, p 49).

F

Text

Clutter and extreme hoarding are facets of the broader issue of self-neglect. A simple definition of this is one of the refusal or impotence of an individual to safely manage and maintain their personal health, safety and well-being; this may be characterised in many ways including the maintenance of a safe living environment.

(Britten and Whitby, 2018, pp 10–11)

Paraphrase

Britten and Whitby _____ self-neglect as 'the refusal or impotence of an individual to safely manage and maintain their personal health, safety and well-being; this may be characterised in many ways including the maintenance of a safe living environment' (2018, pp 10–11).

Academic malpractice

Academic malpractice includes any practice whereby a student attempts to gain credit that they do not deserve. Academic malpractice is a disciplinary offence in almost all universities and it can have severe consequences. The most common types of academic malpractice are:

- **plagiarism** – using the ideas, work or words of others without clear acknowledgement;
- **collusion** – hiding the contribution of others in your work;
- **falsification** – or fabrication of results.

Most written assignments are screened using software such as **Turnitin**. Turnitin alerts lecturers to possible instances of plagiarism or collusion. Work that shows a significant match with the literature or with an essay by another student will be closely scrutinised by assessors. Serious and/or repeated incidences of plagiarism/collusion will be penalised (a mark of zero is typical, sometimes without an option to resubmit) and may also lead to a disciplinary hearing.

Avoiding academic malpractice is especially important in those studying for a professional qualification, as professional bodies (eg the HCPC) insist on a person's integrity if they are to enter, or remain on, the appropriate professional register. To enter and remain on the HCPC Register, a person needs to be of good health and good character, and intentional academic malpractice is likely to be seen an impediment to good character.

Just as if you were a qualified social worker, charges of malpractice while a student are likely to lead to you being hauled before a disciplinary or 'Fitness to Practice' committee and you could be expelled from the university – and your professional course – if found guilty. These committees are very formal and tend to include the presence of very senior members of the university, and even lawyers.

Top tips

Avoiding plagiarism

Plagiarism can be a result of someone's clear intention to cheat, but often it can arise from a misunderstanding of academic culture and referencing conventions. Always remember the following.

- Acknowledge the sources of *all* information and ideas, whether directly quoted or paraphrased. References are a good thing: they show you have researched the topic, and, used well, they don't detract from your ideas or originality, they enhance them.

- Overuse of quotation can be seen as a type of plagiarism, and it is certainly a symptom of uncritical use of sources. Only quote something if it is particularly interesting or powerful. Think about using effective words and phrases, integrated into your own words, rather than a whole sentence.

- The more you explain and interpret the literature, and the more you integrate it into your own argument and use it to suit your own writing purpose, the less likely you are to plagiarise. Plagiarism is more likely to occur with a 'patchwork' presentation of sources.

Summary

This chapter has explained why and how you should reference. It has outlined the main features of the Harvard system of referencing, and highlighted some common problems encountered by students. It has guided you towards using sources in a critical way to enhance your own writing, and it has examined the issue of academic malpractice and suggested strategies which can help you to avoid it.

Sources of example texts

Britten, S and Whitby, K (2018) *Self-neglect: A Practical Approach to Risks and Strengths Assessment.* St Albans: Critical Publishing.

Lingen-Stallard, A, Furber, C and Lavender, T (2016) Testing HIV Positive in Pregnancy: A Phenomenological Study of Women's Experiences. *Midwifery*, 35, 31–8.

Musson, P (2017) *Making Sense of Theory and its Application to Social Work Practice*. St Albans: Critical Publishing.

Pryjmachuk, S, Graham, T, Haddad, M and Tylee, A (2011) School Nurses' Perspectives on Managing Mental Health Problems in Children and Young People. *Journal of Clinical Nursing*, 21, 850–9. [online] Available at: www.ncbi.nlm.nih.gov/pubmed/21883575 (accessed 15 May 2017).

Taylor, G (2015) Exposure to Other Fields of Nursing. In Burns, D (ed) *Foundations of Adult Nursing*. London: Sage.

Young, A, Ferguson-Coleman, E and Keady, J (2016) *Understanding Dementia: Effective Information Access from the Deaf Community's Perspective*. Health and Social Care in the Community, 24(1), 39–47.

References

Beirerter, C and Scardamalia, M (1987) *The Psychology of Written Composition*. Hillsdale, NJ: Lawrence Erlbaum.

Chapter 4
Language in use

Learning outcomes

After reading this chapter you will:

- have gained knowledge of academic style;

- have developed strategies for improving the clarity of your writing;

- be able to distinguish between formal and informal language with confidence;

- have gained knowledge of useful grammar and punctuation rules and patterns in academic writing;

- be able to avoid some common errors in academic writing.

This chapter provides information and strategies to help develop your control of language for the purpose of academic writing. It will help you to write clearly, and to produce writing which is accurate and academic in style.

Reflection

1) What do you understand by 'academic style'?
2) What challenges do you face when you try to write in an academic style?
3) Are there any aspects of grammar, spelling and punctuation that you struggle with?
4) What resources do you use to help you with writing?

Academic style

You will hear a lot about 'academic style' and 'academic writing' at university. It can sometimes feel as if you are expected to learn a new language, or a different version of the English you know. This can be intimidating, especially if you do not have a lot of recent experience in writing academic essays, or if English is not your first language. Of course, it is necessary to adopt an appropriate style at university, particularly in writing, but there is nothing mysterious about this style. In fact, it could be said to have just three basic characteristics:

- it is clear and easy to read;
- it is concise and precise;
- it is formal in expression.

CROSS
REFERENCE

Chapter 2,
Coherent
texts and
arguments

Clarity

The information, ideas and arguments you are required to present in academic essays may be very complex. It is therefore particularly important that the language you use to communicate these things is as clear and readable as possible. As mentioned above, many factors contribute to clarity, some of which will be discussed in this section, some of which are covered in other parts of this book. Clarity and coherence, in particular, are inextricably linked, so you will find many cross references to Chapter 2.

Task

Clarity

Read the two paragraphs below and decide which is clearer and easier to read.

A

As McGrandels and Duffy (2012) point out, a degree of anxiety and worry is a normality for most people, who will feel anxiety at some point in their lives. People feel stressed and the heart rate increases and blood pressure rises and there is diversion of blood to the muscles for 'fight or flight' initiation, like running away. People are careful and prepared for dealing with short-term menacing threats and difficult emergencies (Wilkinson, 2005) and there is enhancement of energy from a rise in blood sugar from a release of a chemical called cortisol into the blood stream by the adrenal glands.

B

As McGrandels and Duffy (2012) point out, a degree of anxiety is normal and most people will experience anxiety at some point in their lives. Anxiety and stress can initiate protective mechanisms in the body which prepare us for 'fight of flight'. When this happens, the heart rate increases, blood pressure rises, and blood is diverted to the muscles to help us respond to the threat, by running away, for example. Cortisol is also released into the blood stream by the adrenal glands, and this has the effect of raising blood sugar in order to enhance energy. The result of this response is increased vigilance and a preparedness to deal with short-term threats and emergencies (Wilkinson, 2005).

Discussion: clarity

Text B is taken (in a slightly adapted form) from a widely used textbook (Taylor, 2015, p 168). You probably found it easier to read than Text A. There are a number of reasons for this.

- Overall, Text B **flows**, whereas Text A is meandering and disjointed, and the reader has to work hard to extract any sense from it. Text B is kinder to the reader: it moves from a general statement in the first sentence to specific details.

It explains a complex process step by step, whereas A jumps around from one part of the process to another in a random fashion. In B, the stages are logically ordered and clearly linked, in this case reflecting real-life biological processes. Linking words such as 'also' in B are a way of making connections explicit.

- It is common in English writing to refer back to the main theme of the previous sentence before introducing new information. This can be seen in B, in the use of the word 'anxiety' in the first sentence and then at the start of the second sentence, and in the use of the phrases 'when this happens' and 'the result of this response' later in the text; 'this/these' are commonly used to refer back in a text.

- Text B uses repetition to help the reader. For example, as noted above, the second sentence repeats the word 'anxiety' from the first sentence; Text A breaks this link and starts talking about people feeling 'stressed', which is a slightly different point. In A, the reader gets confused, or has to make a connection for themselves, and no reader should have to work that hard!

- Text B has shorter sentences which contain a manageable amount of information; Text A sometimes tries to cover too much information in a single sentence, and it overuses the word 'and' to connect ideas in a very loose way.

- Text B uses simple, direct language: 'normal', rather than 'normality'; 'blood is diverted' rather than 'there is diversion of blood'; 'to deal with' rather than 'for dealing with'; 'to enhance' rather than 'there is enhancement of'.

- Text B is concise. It does not include unnecessary words or phrases. In A, there is redundancy, ie the use of two or more words which actually mean the same or very similar things ('anxiety and worry'), and the inclusion of words which are unnecessary because they do not add meaning ('threats' are by definition 'menacing'; 'emergencies' imply 'difficulty').

- Text B uses more precise expression. We conventionally 'experience' – rather than 'have' – anxiety, and the word 'vigilant' (being careful to look out for particular dangers) carries much more specific meaning than the rather vague 'careful'.

Strategies for achieving clarity

From the previous discussion of the two texts, it is clear that there are certain strategies that you can adopt to help you produce clearer writing.

1) Order ideas and sentences in a logical, step-by-step manner, moving from **general to specific** information and ideas.

2) Consider if it will help the reader if you **link back** to the previous sentence before introducing new information, possibly using 'this/these'.

3) Use sensible **repetition** to remind the reader of what is being discussed. This can be seen as a kind of 'lucid repetition' because of how it may facilitate the brain's ability to process information (McIntyre, 1997); note that this is quite different from redundancy, where words or information are repeated for no good reason, often because the text is insufficiently controlled.

4) Do not be afraid of using **short sentences** and **simple language** where these help you communicate difficult ideas clearly. Most academic writing contains a

CROSS REFERENCE

Chapter 2, Coherent texts and arguments, General and specific information

CROSS REFERENCE

Chapter 2, Coherent texts and arguments, Old and new information mixture of short and long sentences, but it is important that long sentences are carefully constructed, and that they are not just chains of phrases linked by 'and' or 'but'.

5) Be **concise**. Avoid redundancy and wordiness – throwing down words on the page for their own sake does not make something more academic! Also, remember that you will be required to meet strict word counts in your essays.

6) Be **precise**. Choose words and expressions very carefully so that they convey the exact message you intend. Check that your expression is not vague or ambiguous.

Task

Being concise

 Cross out any unnecessary words (ie words which are redundant or which do not add meaning) in the text below.

It was in 1864 that teacher and artist Octavia Hill (1838–1912) first started to work in the poorer neighbourhoods of late Victorian inner London (in what is now the borough of Marylebone, which is in inner London and nowadays is one of the most expensive places to live in the capital). She worked with people at the bottom of the social ladder: the poor, unemployed, those who couldn't find work, all living in cold and damp London dwellings. Housing was her main concern. Hill believed that a well maintained home, however small or compact, with light, air and space – with neighbours who care about each other – is one of life's main necessities.

(Adapted from History of Social Work, https://historyof socialwork.org/eng/details.php?cps=3)

Task

Being precise

Choose the word or phrase which conveys the most precise meaning in the sentences below.

1) Since Octavia Hill first began her pioneering work in 1864, social work has grown/evolved into a highly skilled profession.

2) Interventions with carers are meant to be empowering experiences rather than being unnecessarily invasive/intrusive encounters.

3) The study surveyed social workers to determine/decide their reasons for entering the profession.

4) Service users having/exhibiting symptoms of post-natal depression were referred to the community health support group.

5) Psychiatrists will administer/give drugs at the local rehabilitation centre.

6) The study reports on a simple <u>diagnosis/diagnostic</u> test for post-natal depression.

7) Improved community service delivery has a high impact <u>for/in terms of</u> patient satisfaction.

8) The report details the side effects <u>of/associated with</u> the treatment.

Top tips

Being precise

Avoid using 'etc' or 'and so on'. Also avoid ending sentences with ellipsis (…). Instead use 'such as' or 'for example/for instance' with two or three concrete examples.

The study looks into the factors affecting parent–child attachment – parental sensitivity and style, infant temperament etc.

> → The study looks into the factors affecting parent–child attachment such as parental sensitivity and style and infant temperament.

Formality

Everybody changes their language to suit the situation they are in: they speak politely and carefully in a job interview; they use relaxed – or sometimes colourful – language among friends; the tone of their emails varies, depending on the recipient.

Task

Identifying formal style

Look at the texts below and decide if they are formal or informal. What is the purpose of each text? Who do you think is the target reader?

A

Postpartum (or puerperal) psychosis is a severe episode of mental illness representing a psychiatric emergency, with a sudden onset during the days or weeks following childbirth. (Royal College of Psychiatrists, 2014). It is more serious than postnatal depression and can present in different ways. Affected women may have very rapid changes in mood, including symptoms of depression or mania (Royal College of Psychiatrists, 2014). A woman with postpartum psychosis may not be able to care for herself or her baby.

(Taylor, 2015, p 146)

B

Imagine looking at your newborn baby and being convinced they are the son of God. You may think this recent plotline in EastEnders sounds far-fetched.

But it's actually a common symptom of post-partum psychosis, a condition that affects one in 500 mothers. "It's like being in a vivid nightmare only you don't wake up," says psychiatrist Dr Alain Gregoire, at the Winchester Mother and Baby Unit.

(Bates, 2016)

C

Postpartum psychosis (PP) is a serious, but rare, diagnosis occurring in around one in 1000 births. You're likely to experience a mix of:

- depression
- mania
- psychosis

Symptoms usually start quite suddenly within a few weeks after giving birth. PP is sometimes called puerperal psychosis. Postpartum psychosis can be an overwhelming and frightening experience for you and your loved ones, and it's important to seek help as soon as possible. With the right support, most women fully recover.

(Mind, no date)

Discussion: identifying formal style

Text A is taken from an academic textbook. Text B is taken from an online magazine. Text C is from the Mind mental health charity website.

- Text A is objective and impersonal, as its principal aim is to inform a scholarly reader. The language is formal and technical ('severe episode'; 'sudden onset'; 'present'). It uses cautious language to avoid overgeneralisation ('can present'; 'may have'; 'may not be able'). The factual content is supported by reference to academic sources, presented according to academic conventions.

- Text B is very personal and colourful, as one of its principal aims is to engage the attention of a general, non-expert reader and keep their interest. It contains popular cultural references (son of God; EastEnders). It has informal grammar and punctuation (starting a sentence with an imperative – 'Imagine'; starting a sentence with 'But'; the use of personal pronouns – 'your newborn baby', 'you may'; the use of contractions – 'it's'). It contains conversational language ('actually'). It uses a lot of direct quotation and a lot of in-text detail about the source of the information, but it is lacking formal academic references – there is no evidential support for the claim about the number of mothers affected (and the number it gives differs from the figure given by Mind).

- Text C is neither very formal nor very informal in tone. Its aim is to inform and educate the general public, so it is generally clear and accessible to a non-expert reader. The language is mostly neutral and factual, but it is also personal and conversational, addressing the reader as 'you', and using contractions ('it's', 'you're'). Most of the vocabulary is neutral, apart from 'around', which is slightly informal, and 'loved ones', which has an emotional overtone. These less formal features give it a softer, almost comforting tone, while the generally neutral and factual style invites trust. The text also differs from the academic text in that it does not provide any evidence for the figure it provides on the numbers affected.

The formal style that characterises Text A (and parts of C) will be discussed in this section, and there will be guidance on how to avoid some of the informal features in Text B (and parts of C).

Other characteristics of academic writing such as the use of cautious language to indicate stance, and the role of references are discussed in other chapters of this book.

CROSS REFERENCE

Chapter 3, Referring to sources

Task

Word choice

Look at the words below. What do they have in common? What differentiates them?

> minor, juvenile, paediatric, kid, bairn, brat, suckling, offspring, infant, child

Discussion: word choice

These are all words associated with children, but they differ in terms of style and common usage. Language style can be broadly categorised as follows:

FORMAL	NEUTRAL	INFORMAL
infant	child	kid

Formal language can include specialised or technical terms, for example, scientific words such as 'offspring', and legal words such as 'minor' and 'juvenile'. In medical fields, the specialised term 'paediatric', relating to the management of conditions affecting children, is commonly used.

So context is everything, and the university context requires specific language use. The language of academic writing can be neutral or formal, and it often includes specialised or technical terms. You must be careful to avoid informal, colloquial language like 'kid', including dialect words like 'bairn' (used in Scotland and some areas of Northern England), and slang words, especially those with derogatory associations, such as 'brat'. Dictionaries often provide information on the special characteristics of words.

CROSS REFERENCE

Appendix 1, English language references

CROSS
REFERENCE

Appendix 1,
English
language
references

Top tips

Using a thesaurus

A thesaurus can be a useful tool, but like any tool, it requires careful use. You should avoid unthinking reliance on the information it provides: the terms listed in a thesaurus as synonyms are often not exact synonyms, and there is often a lack of information on the style or usage of the term. For example, a thesaurus may provide the following synonyms for the word 'old':

> elderly, geriatric, senile, aged, ancient, decrepit, venerable, hoary, over the hill

CROSS
REFERENCE

Chapter 2,
Coherent
texts and
arguments,
Referring
back in the
text: repetition,
variation and
pronoun use

However, only the first three are appropriate for academic use, and even they have very specific uses: 'elderly' is more respectful than 'old'; 'geriatric' is a technical term common in medical use; 'senile' can refer to the loss of mental faculties (though it can also be used in an insulting way in everyday slang). The other words would sound inappropriate, strange or disturbing in an academic essay or social work notes!

Before you use a word you have never used before, check in a good dictionary to find out information on usage and to see authentic examples containing the word. And remember that a synonym may not be the best choice; repeating the same word may help the reader more.

Also, note that some terms used in a healthcare and social care environment may not even feature in a general thesaurus, for example, the term 'later life', which is a positive term commonly used in relation to elderly people.

> Training in later life care is available to staff.
>
> Gentle exercise can facilitate mobility in later life.

It is clear that some words should be avoided completely. However, a lot of language use is a matter of choice. You can often choose between a neutral word and a more formal word. Both will often be acceptable in an academic essay, but the more formal choice may well enhance your writing.

Task

Identifying inappropriate language

 Cross out the terms in the lists below which would be inappropriate in an academic essay because they are too informal or literary. It may be necessary to consult a dictionary for one or two of the words.

1) male/man/bloke

2) inebriated/tipsy/drunk

3) impecunious/poor/broke

4) food/nutrition/grub

5) sleep/slumber/doze

Task

Identifying formal language

Identify the more formal choice in the sentences below.

1) <u>Not much/Little</u> research has been carried out on the topic of how the learning styles of students impacts on their experience within practice learning environments.

2) The situation for homeless young people <u>deteriorated/got worse</u> following the closure of local hostels and support services.

3) In 2018, a social worker, Al Coates, <u>got/was awarded</u> an MBE in recognition of his services to children.

4) Children and families social workers have an average caseload of <u>about/approximately</u> 18 open cases.

5) Social workers are required to <u>adhere/keep</u> to the HCPC standards of conduct, performance and ethics.

6) It is essential that social workers <u>show/demonstrate</u> a capacity for empathy and compassion.

7) It is important to <u>ensure/make</u> sure that students are provided with high quality practice learning placements.

8) There are many ways service users and carers can contribute to social work programmes <u>such as/like</u> interviewing social work candidates at interview.

9) Serious Case Reviews frequently recommend that inter-professional relationships need to <u>get better/improve</u> to ensure key information is appropriately shared across relevant agencies.

10) A range of therapies can be employed to relieve pain and <u>facilitate/help</u> the healing process.

11) <u>More and more/An increasing number</u> of local authorities are looking to attract newly qualified social workers into supported ASYE posts.

12) There are <u>a lot of/many</u> studies on the experiences of young people in the care system.

Strategies for making your writing more formal

1) Avoid conversational expressions such as 'actually', 'by the way' or 'to be honest'.

2) Use the formal negatives, 'little/few', rather than the more conversational 'not much/not many':

little time/concern/appreciation (uncountable nouns)

few adoptive families/specialist therapists/tailored services (countable nouns)

3) It is grammatically correct to start a sentence with 'and' or 'but', and you will find sentences like this in academic texts. However, if you start too many sentences with these words, your style will seem too chatty and unstructured, so make good use of more formal options such as 'in addition' and 'however'.

4) Place adverbs before the main verb (rather than at the beginning or the end of a sentence, as is common in spoken English):

Originally, the online research programme was developed for qualifying social workers.

→ The online research programme was originally developed for qualifying social workers.

5) Academic discourse aims to be objective. For this reason, care should be taken with the use of personalised language, including personal pronouns such as 'I/you/ we'. There may be some situations in which you are expected to write in a personal style, for example, in a reflective essay, where you are required to discuss your thought processes etc; also, some academic journals, in medicine and psychology for example, have made the conscious decision to adopt a more direct style (eg the use of 'we', as in sentences such as 'We selected fifty samples', instead of passive constructions like 'Fifty samples were selected'). It is therefore necessary to consider each situation in isolation before making a choice about the type of language required. As far as academic assignments are concerned, most will require you to use impersonal structures such as those below:

You can see a comparison of service user outcomes in Table 2.

→ A comparison of service user outcomes can be seen in Table 2.

I think this approach is preferable.

→ There is evidence to support this approach (Cross, 2011; Turner, 2015).

6) Avoid contractions like 'they're', 'he's' and 'can't'. You will find contractions in many academic textbooks (occasionally in this one), as the writers want to make them accessible, but they are not felt to be appropriate in academic essays or scholarly journals.

CROSS
REFERENCE

Colons

7) Be cautious with informal punctuation such as dashes (–) and exclamation marks (!). Dashes are sometimes used as a type of parenthesis (as an alternative to brackets), but colons can often provide a more formal alternative:

Co-production ensures that citizens or decision makers – or people who use services, family carers and service providers – all contribute to the decision.

→ Co-production ensures that all relevant parties contribute to the decision: citizens or decision makers, people who use services, family carers and service providers.

(Adapted from Britten and Whitby, 2018, 35)

Task

Improving style

 Rewrite the text below so that it is more formal and academic in style.

The aging population means that more and more people have to be carers and a lot of them are struggling. They often don't get help and they're facing cuts in the benefits and services they can get. We can see from lots of studies that the well-being of carers gets worse the more hours of care they give. A great partnership with professionals will make outcomes for both carers and patients much better. All professionals – social workers, doctors, district nurses, general practice nurses – should respect carers as expert partners in care. And social workers need to have certain values and skills – eg compassion, competence, commitment – to make sure carers' overall well-being is looked after.

Top tips

Using the Academic Word List

The **Academic Word List** (Coxhead, 2000) is a list of words which have a high frequency in English-language academic texts. The words at the top end of the list, ie the most frequent, include:

> analyse, approach, area, assume, benefit, concept, consistent, context, data, established, evidence, factor, identified, indicate, involved, issue, major, method, occur, procedure, process, role, significant, specific, theory, variable

You can check if a word you want to use is on the list at: www.victoria.ac.nz/lals/resources/academicwordlist/

Grammar, spelling and punctuation

When lecturers read and assess your work, they are not looking for perfection. They will overlook occasional minor errors, as long as they do not interfere with the readability of the text or obscure the meaning. However, it is very hard to get high marks if there are numerous grammar, spelling or punctuation errors in your writing, even if the content is good. The standard of your English also has implications for professional practice. Social work students, for BA and MA programmes, need to pass a written test to confirm their literacy before being accepted onto qualifying social work programmes.

CROSS REFERENCE

Communication Skills for your Social Work Degree

CROSS
REFERENCE

Appendix 2,
Grammatical
terminology

English grammar, spelling and punctuation can be a challenge both for students whose first language is not English and for some native speakers. In the UK, educational attitudes towards the explicit teaching of grammar to school children have varied greatly over the last few decades. Whatever the rights and wrongs of this, one of the outcomes is that some people in the UK may have learned very little about grammar at school. And even those who did may feel a bit hazy about some of the rules and terminology. In order to meet the standards necessary for academic success, it is necessary to grasp certain grammatical concepts. This section provides explanations and examples which will help students who lack confidence in this area. You will find more detailed explanations and examples of grammatical terms used in this chapter (in **bold** in the text) in Appendix 2.

CROSS
REFERENCE

Chapter 5,
Preparing
your work for
submission,
Editing and
proofreading
your final text

Sometimes, errors are down to insufficient proofreading, rather than a lack of knowledge. It is essential that you leave yourself enough time to read through your finished essay or report several times, firstly to make sure that it is readable and makes sense, and secondly to proofread and pick up 'typos' (typing errors), grammar, spelling and punctuation slips, or messy formatting.

Common areas of difficulty in grammar and spelling

There are a number of areas of grammar and spelling that cause particular problems.

Quantifiers

Quantifiers are words used before **nouns** (terms used for people, places or things) to indicate number or amount.

- The quantifier 'fewer' is used with **countable nouns** (literally things which can be counted, usually ending in 's' in English):

  less social workers/respite care opportunities/day centres ✗

  fewer social workers/respite care opportunities/day centres ✓

- The quantifier 'less' is used with **uncountable nouns** (things seen as a mass which cannot be split or counted):

  less injustice/discrimination/unhappiness

- The quantifier 'amount' should only be used with uncountable nouns:

  a large amount of Mental Health social workers ✗

  a large number of Mental Health social workers ✓

  a large amount of distress ✓

Grammatical agreement

- Most **sentences** in English contain a **main clause** which is built upon two basic elements: a **subject**, and a **verb** which agrees with it:

  The meeting [subject] was [verb] insightful.

Many of the local authorities mentioned in the select committee's report [subject] are situated [verb] in areas of high deprivation.

Be careful to make sure a verb agrees with its subject; it is quite easy to get this wrong if the main word in the subject and the verb are far apart, and if there are other nouns between the subject and verb:

One of the most difficult challenges faced by student social workers during their practice placements are also having to keep up with academic study requirements. ✗

One of the most difficult challenges faced by student social workers during their practice placements is also having to keep up with academic study requirements. ✓

- **Nouns** can sometimes be replaced with **pronouns** (short words such as 'he/it/them'). These pronouns must also agree with the noun they refer to:

Information is supplied on the assessments and on how it is undertaken. ✗

Information is supplied on the assessments and on how they are undertaken. ✓

Commonly confused words

Many errors in students' written work arise because of confusion between certain words.

- Be careful to distinguish between 'there' and 'their'. The former introduces the theme of the sentence, or signifies place; the latter denotes possession:

There are a number of issues affecting how carers respond to offers of support.

It is helpful if carers are explicit about their own support needs.

- Do not confuse 'effect' (noun) and 'affect' (verb):

The quality of supervision provided in agencies can have a profound **effect** on social workers and people who use their services.

The quality of supervision provided in agencies can **affect** both social workers and people who use their services profoundly.

There is a verb 'effect', but it has another meaning (to make happen, bring about), and is usually restricted to particular nouns such as 'change':

A number of community-based social workers reported that the changes in service organisation left them feeling more powerful to **effect** change in their organisation.

- Be careful to distinguish between **singular** and **plural** with the following words:

a recent phenomenon (singular)

the study of several phenomena important to social work research (plural)

provide evidence of practice related to each criterion (singular)

meet all the criteria (plural)

CROSS REFERENCE

Chapter 2, Coherent texts and arguments, Referring back in the text: repetition, variation and pronoun use

- Differentiate between the following **noun** and **verb** spellings:

NOUN –*ICE*	VERB –*ISE*
advice	advise
device	devise
practice	practise
licence	license

Task

Commonly confused words

 Choose the correct form of the word in the sentences below.

1) New government policy has implications for social work <u>practice/practise</u>.

2) The policy affects the ability of social workers to <u>practice/practise</u> in a person-centred way.

3) Carers were offered <u>advice/advise</u> on available support.

4) Social workers can <u>advice/advise</u> on how to access community resources.

5) The social worker asked the occupational therapist whether there was a <u>device/devise</u> for helping Mrs Andrews with her cooking when she returned home.

6) A global definition of social work has been <u>deviced/devised</u> by the International Federation of Social Workers.

7) Within the United States of America social workers need to be <u>licenced/licensed</u> to practice.

8) Applicants must possess a valid driving <u>licence/license</u>.

9) The paper reported on the <u>affects/effects</u> of the drug.

10) A number of service users were <u>affected/effected</u> by the changes in eligibility criteria.

11) The social work students started on <u>there/their</u> first practice placement in October.

12) <u>There/Their</u> is a strong case for supporting families in crisis.

Note that US English uses 'practice' and 'license' for both noun and verb.

Common areas of difficulty in punctuation

There are some strict rules governing punctuation in English; these rules are largely tied up with English grammar rules, such as the use of commas with relative clauses (discussed later in this section). However, in other cases, there are choices available to you; these choices are a question of style, but they are still important as they can affect clarity and readability. Some important punctuation rules and choices are discussed below.

The apostrophe

If you have problems with apostrophes, you are not alone! David Crystal, a well-known linguistics scholar, cites apostrophe use as one of the most problematic aspects of the English language: 'Another day when the phone doesn't stop ringing, and (once again) all because of the apostrophe' (Crystal, 2012). It is a topic which clearly exercises the general British public, judging by the number of letters sent to newspapers to complain of apostrophe misuse! However, there are some simple rules which can help.

- After a **singular noun**, or a **proper noun** (like a name), **'s** is used to denote possession:

    in this service user's best interests

    The Department for Education's Knowledge and Skills Statements for Child and Family Social Work

    After **plural nouns**, and **proper nouns** ending in **s**, the apostrophe comes after the **s**:

    in these service users' best interests

    Mayer and Timms' classic text, *The Client Speaks*

    It is also acceptable to add a possessive **s** in this case, as in 'Burns's book', but be consistent. Be careful with irregular plurals not ending in s – the apostrophe comes before the possessive **s**.

    the children's parents

- Apostrophes also signal missing letters in **contractions** like 'can't' (cannot), 'doesn't' (does not) and 'they'll' (they will).

    Do not confuse words which sound the same but have different meanings, grammar and spelling:

    — 'it's' is the contracted form of 'it is/has', whereas 'its' is a **possessive pronoun** like 'my' or 'her':

        The voluntary organisation provided details of <u>its</u> policy on staff development.

        <u>It's</u> hot today.

    — 'your' is a possessive pronoun, while 'you're' is a contraction of 'you are'.

        Always write <u>your</u> student number on the front cover of your essays.

        <u>You're</u> late.

— 'they're' is a contraction of 'they are', distinct from 'there' and 'their'

There is pressure on local councils to stay within their budgets.

They're here!

You will avoid this problem if you write, as you should, without using contractions.

Hyphens

Multi-word **adjectives** (words which describe nouns), such as the first word of this sentence, are usually hyphenated when they come before a noun, but not when they come after:

an out-of-date social work text book

a social work textbook which is out of date

a three-day-old baby

a baby who is three days old

Brackets

Brackets should be used sparingly as they can interrupt the flow of a text. If you do use them, be aware of the rules.

- If the bracketed information is part of the sentence, it requires no specific punctuation:

    The data (collected over a three-month period) revealed a significant improvement in the number of users visiting the project.

The brackets here could be replaced with commas or perhaps dashes (though dashes are a little on the informal side).

- If the brackets contain a separate sentence, it should be punctuated as such:

    The data revealed a significant improvement in the number of users visiting the project. (The data was collected over a three-month period.) Many users commented on the positive impact of additional transport being provided.

    In cases like this, brackets are just one choice available for reducing the focus on this piece of information. Other choices include:

    The data, which was collected over a three-month period, revealed a significant improvement in the number of users visiting the project.

Punctuation and sentence structure

The use of full stops, commas, colons and semi-colons is intrinsically linked with the control of sentence structure in English. Some of the most important rules and patterns are detailed below.

Full stops

Full stops are the most straightforward of punctuation marks and they do not really cause problems for students (although their misuse is linked with 'fragments' and 'run-ons', discussed later in this section). Suffice it to say that they are the main way of indicating the boundaries between **sentences**.

Over recent years the world of social care, particularly in relation to work with adults, has changed dramatically. These changes have seen a shift from a focus upon social workers as the commissioners of packages of care, to more full re-engagement with the professional values of empowerment, autonomy and person-centred control.

(Britten and Whitby, 2018, p 1)

Commas

Commas are the equivalent of changing gear when driving; you come to a point where you need to slow down a little or turn a corner. The commas help you negotiate these changes, but also, and perhaps more importantly, they enable you to take your reader along with you.

(Peck and Coyle, 2012, p 54)

So commas can be a way of guiding, or 'driving', your reader through the text. Below are some common patterns in comma use.

- It can make a sentence easier to read if the parts of a **sentence** which come before, after, or in the middle of the main idea are separated with commas, especially in longer sentences:

> Social work is diverse and there are many career paths you can travel. One thing is for certain, you'll never get bored, and each area is full of its own challenges and opportunities, whether in the voluntary, public or private sector.
>
> (Adams and Sheard, 2017, p 9)

> Social workers need to have a good understanding of the principles of charging, in particular what can and cannot be charged for.
>
> (Feldon, 2017, p 102)

> The concept and application of a risks and strengths approach in cases of self-neglect is a complex area in social work practice, with many varying facets interwoven together.
>
> (Britten and Whitby, 2018, p 70)

> If adult mental health is the Cinderella of health service provision, in terms of the amount of taxpayers' money spent as a proportion of overall health care, then child and adolescent mental health must be one of the mice pulling the crystal coach.
>
> (Walker, 2013 p 103)

These commas are not obligatory, and some people prefer not to use them too much as they believe they 'clutter up' the text. When you have a choice like this, let it be motivated by sensitivity to the experience of the reader. Will a comma help the reader navigate the text more easily and focus on the most important information in the sentence?

- It is not obligatory to use a comma before 'and/but/or' when using them to join words or parts of a sentence, but it can often help to make long sentences easier to read. Again, be sensitive to the experience of the reader. In the first example below, the comma before 'but' helps break up a complex sentence with many grammatical elements into two discernible ideas; in the second example, commas signal the three items in the list introduced by the colon ('giving', 'managing', 'involving'), the second 'and' thus clearly forming part of the third item:

> Traditionally, residential social work was seen as a less attractive career pathway in comparison to field-based social work, but in reality it is a rewarding and challenging area of practice that often involves intensive therapeutically based work with some of the most vulnerable people in our society.

> As a hospital-based social worker, you will need to be proactive in involving older people in decisions about their lives from the onset: giving explanations about care packages available upon discharge, managing expectations about what services might be provided and involving families in decision making and home discharge planning.

- The **main clause** (the main idea in a sentence) is usually separated with a comma from a **participle clause** (an '–ing' or '–ed' verb form adding information). This comma is not obligatory, but it can help the reader to follow a long sentence:

> All social workers need to be able to work effectively across professional and agency boundaries, actively engaging in inter-professional work

- Another clause can also be added to a **main clause** with a linking **conjunction** such as 'although/because/whilst'. These two parts of the sentence can be separated with a comma, especially when the main clause follows the other clause:

> While depression is often discussed in relation to adult mental health, children can also be affected.

- Commas are not used before **that-clauses** (structures following certain verbs etc):

> Westwood (2014) recognises, that codes of conduct have been developed in response to concerns about professional boundaries. ✘
> Westwood (2014) recognises that codes of conduct have been developed in response to concerns about professional boundaries. ✓
>
> (Westwood, 2014, p 18)

- Do not use commas directly in between a **subject** and **verb**, no matter how long the subject:

> The assessment of a person's capacity to give or withhold consent, is considered in relation to a specific decision. ✘
> The assessment of a person's capacity to give or withhold consent is considered in relation to a specific decision. ✓
>
> (Tierney et al, 2015, p 345)

Task

Variation in comma use

The two texts below are well written and do not break any punctuation rules. However, they differ in their use of commas. This may be due to individual choice, or editorial policy (they are both from textbooks).

What differences in comma use can you find? Which style do you prefer? Why?

A

The assessment of a person's capacity to give or withhold consent is considered in relation to a specific decision. While the individual may not have capacity to make some decisions they may still retain capacity for other decisions. For example a patient may not have capacity to make a decision regarding a surgical procedure but could retain capacity to consent (or not) to having their clinical observations (eg blood pressure) checked.

(Tierney et al, 2015, p 345)

B

On the face of it, we have found broad support for the ideals of collaborative ways of managing psychiatric medication across all key stakeholder groups. A non-specific conceptualisation of SDM, where individual decisions are part of a longer-term and adaptable process, similar to that proposed by other authors (Entwistle and Watt, 2006; Montori et al, 2006), is widely supported by care co-ordinators, CPNs, psychiatrists and service users in these findings. Service users acknowledge and value more guidance in times of crisis, and strongly believe that SDM can only happen in the context of walking a journey together in a trusting, supportive and honest long-term relationship with a practitioner.

(Kaminskiy et al, 2013, pp 43–4)

Colons

Colons are used to introduce something that expands in some way on what precedes it, by, for example, providing an explanation, or listing items:

> Blogs are a personal opinion and view of an issue, the existence of which encourages the reader to question and engage in a critical appreciation of the content of the blog. See for example this blog which is written by a social work practitioner who is highly critical of the bureaucratic nature of local authority social work in this post: www.hownottodosocialwork.wordpress.com.
>
> (McKendrick, 2014, p 56)

CROSS REFERENCE

Parallel structures

Semi-colons

A semi-colon can be used instead of a full stop to separate **sentences** which are closely connected.

CROSS
REFERENCE

Parallel
structures

Faced with these powerful forces it is natural to defend oneself; these defences have the aim of protecting therapists from the fear of adolescent pain, especially the painfulness of change and separation.

(Brigg, 2017, p 108)

Focus on fragments and run-on sentences

It has been established that most **sentences** in English contain a **main clause** which contains two basic elements: a **subject** and a **verb** which agrees with it:

Social work [subject] is [verb] a dynamic and changing profession.

Social workers [subject] are [verb] accustomed to dealing with situations of uncertainty and risk.

If a sentence is lacking a main clause, or if a main clause is lacking a subject or a main verb, the sentence is incomplete, ie it is a 'fragment':

While the majority of service users reported only mild anxiety. ✗ (no main clause)

While the majority of service users reported only mild anxiety, a small number were seriously affected. ✓

Social workers integration into local schools and GP practices. ✗ (no verb)

Social workers have been integrated into local schools and GP practices. ✓

Lately, have reported an increase in demand for social work services. ✗ (no subject)

Lately, local authorities have reported an increase in demand for social work services. ✓

If there is more than one subject/verb structure, they should be separated by full stops or semi-colons, or connected (with **conjunctions**, for example). If only a comma is used, it creates a 'run-on sentence', which is grammatically incorrect:

Social workers are integrated into local schools and GP practices, they undertake much needed preventative work. ✗

Social workers are integrated into local schools and GP practices; they undertake much needed preventative work. ✓

Social workers are integrated into local schools and GP practices, and they undertake much needed preventative work. ✓

Run-on sentences also include those beginning with words and phrases used to connect two sentences such as 'however/therefore/as a result':

Research teaching is a central part of undergraduate social work curricula in the UK, however, students sometimes initially struggle to appreciate its importance. ✗

Research teaching is a central part of undergraduate nursing curricula in the UK. However, students sometimes initially struggle to appreciate its importance. ✓

Research teaching is a central part of undergraduate social work curricula in the UK. However, students sometimes initially struggle to appreciate its importance. ✓

Focus on 'hanging participles'

As discussed above, it is common to attach a **participle clause** to a main clause. However, it is important to make sure that the two parts of such a sentence are clearly connected.

Being prone to non-engagement, social workers are required to make additional efforts to engage these service users. ✗

Being prone to non-engagement, these service users require additional efforts to engage them. ✓

Referred with a longstanding history of psychosis, a social worker assessed the service user. ✗

Referred with a longstanding history of psychosis, the service user was assessed by the social worker. ✓

In the examples marked as incorrect, it is as if the social workers are being described by the first clause. This can also happen with other phrases, creating a certain ambiguity in the example below.

Without an understanding of what their stories are about, social workers cannot fully engage with their service users. ✗

Without an understanding of what their stories are about, service users cannot be fully engaged with. ✓

Focus on relative clauses

The pronouns 'that' and 'which' are used to refer back to nouns in what are called 'relative clauses'. These are very common in academic writing because they are very useful for defining terms and adding information to the main topic of a sentence. However, the rules are quite complicated and mistakes are quite common. In brief, 'that' and 'which' can both be used to refer back to something which is being defined or restricted in some way (restrictive/defining relative clauses); 'that' or 'who' are used for people. There are no commas in this case:

Social workers suggested the app as an electronic device that/which can be used to help service users establish an effective online support group. (defining; one type of device)

Specialist training is required for social workers who/that want to work as Approved Mental Health Practitioners. (restricted subset of social workers)

Only 'which' (or 'who' for people) can be used when extra adding information (non-restrictive/non-defining relative clauses) which relates to the whole group or idea, not a subset. This type of clause can be removed from the sentence without making the sentence ungrammatical. Commas must be used in these sentences:

Service users are encouraged to build upon their strengths, which can often facilitate optimism and movement forward.

One type of psychotherapy is cognitive behavioural therapy (CBT), which is used to treat a wide variety of psychological disorders.

Social workers, who work with many people experiencing domestic abuse, are appropriately placed to contribute to public debates on this issue.

Refining grammar and punctuation

Task

Grammar and punctuation

1) Punctuate the text below so that it makes sense.

social factors also seem to influence depression rates depression is more common in the unemployed those living alone those who are divorced or separated those living in local authority or housing association accommodation those with a lower socioeconomic status and or material disadvantage and those with no formal educational qualifications social factors such as isolation racist attacks and dissatisfaction with housing may also contribute to depression in refugee groups indeed in traumatised refugees and asylum seekers poor social support seems to be a stronger predictor of depression in the long term than the severity of the initial trauma

(Adapted from Briddon et al, 2011, p 108)

2) Correct the grammar and punctuation mistakes in the text below.

Postnatal depression effects 10–15 in every 100 woman after childbirth. It can be difficult to detect because it may present different in different women. The symptoms of postnatal depression is similar to that of depression at any other stage of life, the difference is the presence of a baby, that is likely to be the focus of the womans thoughts and difficulties. The disorder maybe mild or severe. Milder forms might be treat within the primary healthcare team. While more severe forms will require additional input from psychiatric services. Diagnosing postnatal depression requires clinical assessment by GP or mental health specialist, however, nursing and midwifery staff, must be alert to the disorder in order make timely referrals.

(Adapted from Taylor, 2015, p 145)

Top tips

Spelling and grammar check

Use a spell and grammar tool, but always double-check that the suggestion given to you makes sense, as these computer programmes cannot recognise some subtleties of usage, especially in grammar. Also, make sure your spell and grammar check is set to UK English, as there are a number of differences between UK and US English, and it is important to be consistent.

	UK	US
–ise v –ize	prioritise, recognise	prioritize, recognize*
–our v –or	colour, behaviour	color; behavior
–re v –er	centre, metre	center, meter
–ll– v –l–	travelling, cancelled	traveling, canceled

*The 'z' spelling is also acceptable in UK English; just be consistent.

Parallel structures

Parallel structures are formed when there is repetition of words, phrases, grammatical structures and punctuation patterns (combined with contrasting elements which move the text forward). They are common in academic writing because they are useful tools for organising information clearly, particularly when comparing and contrasting, or when listing items. Note how these structures often include colons and semi-colons as organisational tools, eg:

> Schön (1983) distinguishes between <u>reflection on action</u> and <u>reflection in action</u>. <u>Reflecting *on* action</u> happens <u>after the event</u>, <u>reflection *in* action</u> <u>during the event</u>. <u>Reflection on action is</u> a prerequisite to becoming <u>a competent practitioner</u>; <u>reflection in action</u>, on the other hand, <u>is</u> a deeper skill that is essential if you are to become <u>a capable practitioner</u>.
>
> (Pryjmachuk, 2011c, p 67)

> There are many reasons adolescents can find emotions difficult to process. Two common reasons are: <u>hormonal changes</u> (<u>which</u> can impact profoundly on mood) and <u>societal expectations</u> (<u>where</u> society expects a higher level of maturity in response than the adolescent is able to offer).
>
> (Gregory, 2015, p 95)

> Physical medicine has made significant progress in dealing with the consequences of trauma, illness and disease: <u>it has cured</u> people of terrible diseases such as small pox; <u>it has enabled</u> people to survive following traumatic injuries; and, through transplantation, <u>it has extended</u> the lives of those with failing organs.
>
> (Pryjmachuk, 2011b, p 12)

Notice how the *repetition* of certain phrases and structures highlights the information which is *different*, eg 'on' vs 'in'; 'capable' vs 'competent'; 'hormonal changes' vs 'societal expectations'. This combination of repetition and change makes the text very easy to process for the reader (McIntyre, 1997).

Be careful to avoid 'faulty parallelism', ie when items in a list do not share the same grammar:

> There are many reasons adolescents can find emotions difficult to process. Two common reasons are: <u>hormonal changes</u> (these impacted profoundly on mood) and <u>what society expects</u> (society had expectations of a higher level of maturity than the adolescent is able to offer). ✗

Task

Parallel structures

Use the notes below to write short texts using parallel structures. Think about how you might use commas, colons and semi-colons to organise the information.

1) recording errors – impact – service user, social worker, organisation

2) initiative – Early Support and Intervention Programme – helps young adults with a diagnosed mental health problem settle into accommodation – aims – help young people manage and keep tenancies/improve living skills, eg budgeting, home and self care/integrate into communities/ promote access to employment, training and education

3) some elderly service users – mobile, eg driving, playing golf/ others – largely sedentary, eg spending a lot of time indoors reading/ watching TV

4) four main theories of explanation social workers draw upon (Musson, 2017) – psychodynamic, behaviourist, systems and radical

Summary

This chapter has analysed elements of academic style and provided strategies to help you write clear, accurate English for academic purposes. It has outlined the choices available to you in terms of expression, grammatical structures and punctuation, as you complete your written assignments. In addition, it has outlined some of the most challenging areas of English grammar and punctuation, in order to help you avoid common errors and refine your writing. Good style and accuracy will help you to create a good impression in your writing, and allow your ideas to shine through.

Sources of example texts

Adams, J and Sheard, A (2017) *Positive Social Work: The Essential Toolkit for NQSWs*. St Albans: Critical Publishing.

Bates, C (2016) 'I Was Convinced that my Baby Would Die the Next Day'. *BBC News Magazine*, 16th February [online]. Available at: www.bbc.co.uk/news/magazine-35543747 (accessed 13 May 2017).

Briddon, J, Baguley, C and Rolfe, L (2011) Helping People Recover from Depression. In Pryjmachuk, S (ed) *Mental Health Nursing: An Evidence-Based Introduction*. London: Sage, 105–46.

Briggs, S (2017) Working with Troubled Adolescents: Observation as a Key Skill for Practitioners. In Hingley-Jones, H, Parkinson, C and Allain, L (eds) *Observations in Health and Social Care: Applications for Learning, Research and Practice with Children and Adults*. London: Jessica Kingsley Publishing.

Britten, S and Whitby, K (2018) *Self-neglect*. St Albans: Critical Publishing.

Feldon, P (2017) *The Social Worker's Guide to the Care Act 2014*. St Albans: Critical Publishing.

Gregory, J (2015) Medicines Management. In Burns, D (ed) *Foundations of Adult Nursing*. London: Sage, 89–108.

Kaminskiy, E, Ramon, S and Morant, N (2013) Exploring Shared Decision-making for Psychiatric Medication Management. In *Modern Mental Health: Critical Perspectives on Psychiatric Practice*. St Albans: Critical Publishing.

McKendrick, D (2014) New Technology in Social Work Education: Blogs and Blogging. In Westwood, J. (Ed) *Social Media in Social Work Education*. St Albans: Critical Publishing

Mind (no date). Postnatal Depression and Perinatal Mental Health. [online] Available at: www.mind.org.uk/information-support/types-of-mental-health-problems/postnatal-depression-and-perinatal-mental-health/postpartum-psychosis/#.WJdNp_mLTIU (accessed 13 May 2017).

Musson, P (2017) *Making Sense of Theory and Its Application to Social Work Practice*. St Albans: Critical Publishing.

Pryjmachuk, S (2011b) Theoretical Perspectives in Mental Health Nursing. In Pryjmachuk, S (ed) *Mental Health Nursing: An Evidence-Based Introduction*. London: Sage, 3–41.

Pryjmachuk, S (2011c) The Capable Mental Health Nurse. In Pryjmachuk, S (ed) *Mental Health Nursing: An Evidence-Based Introduction*. London: Sage, 42–72.

Stanmore, E and Brown Wilson, C (2015) Caring for the Older Person. In Burns, D (ed) *Foundations of Adult Nursing*. London: Sage, 361–94.

Taylor, G (2015) Exposure to Other Fields of Nursing. In Burns, D (ed) *Foundations of Adult Nursing*. London: Sage, 135–78.

Tierney, P, Freeman, S and Gregory, J (2015) Caring for the Acutely Ill Adult. In Burns, D (ed) *Foundations of Adult Nursing*. London: Sage, 313–60.

Walker, S (2013) Culture and Meaning in Child and Adolescent Mental Health. In Walker, S (Ed) *Modern Mental Health: Critical Perspectives on Psychiatric Practice*. St Albans: Critical Publishing.

Westwood, J (2014) Social Media in Social Work Education, St Albans: Critical Publishing.

References

Academic Word List. [online] Available at: www.victoria.ac.nz/lals/resources/academicwordlist (accessed 2 April 2017).

Coxhead, A (2000) A New Academic Wordlist. *TESOL Quarterly*, 34, 213–38.

Crystal, D (2012) On Waterstone(')s. *DCBLOG*. [online] Available at: http://david-crystal.blogspot.co.uk/2012/01/on-waterstones.html (accessed 2 April 2017).

McIntyre, M (1997) Lucidity and Science I: Writing Skills and the Pattern Perception Hypothesis. *Interdisciplinary Science Reviews*, 22, 199–216.

Nursing and Midwifery Council (2015) *The Code: Professional Standards of Practice and Behaviour for Nurses and Midwives*. [online] Available at: www.nmc.org.uk/globalassets/sitedocuments/nmc-publications/nmc-code.pdf (accessed 13 May 2017).

Peck, J and Coyle, M (2012) *Write it Right: The Secrets of Effective Writing*. 2nd ed. New York: Palgrave Macmillan.

Chapter 5
Preparing your work for submission

Learning outcomes

After reading this chapter you will:

- know how to check that the work you submit meets university requirements;

- understand how to edit and proofread your work before submission, and be aware of some of the issues related to this process;

- be able to format and present your work to a high professional standard;

- be aware of some of the writing support available to you at university.

This chapter will help you to assess if a piece of work is ready to be submitted. It offers advice on the final edit of your text, including proofreading. It provides you with information and guidance on formatting and presentation. It also presents the options available to you if you feel you need further professional support with your writing.

Are you ready to submit your work?

When lecturers mark your work, they refer very closely to assessment guidelines and marking descriptors. It is therefore very important that you pay equally close attention to these documents. You should use these as the starting point for your assessment, and as a kind of 'checklist' at the end of the writing process, before you submit. The next section covers some of the most important considerations when preparing your work for submission.

Have you done what you were asked to do?

Checklist

- Have you answered the question or responded to the task in a direct, comprehensive and appropriate way?

- Is the content relevant?

- Have you supported your points and ideas with credible sources and evidence?

- Is your referencing complete, accurate and consistent?

- Have you followed all the guidelines on content, referencing, formatting and presentation to the letter?

Have you stuck to the word count?

You will most certainly be penalised if you either *fail to meet* or *exceed* the specified word count. Word counts are not arbitrary numbers plucked out of the air. They are decided on with a range of factors in mind.

- Word counts ensure equity since all students are given the same limit.
- Written assignments need to be a certain length in order to allow for the inclusion of a substantial amount of detail and/or a substantive argument.
- Word counts can be used to differentiate between different levels of study: for example, a third-year student should be expected to produce more writing on a given topic than a first-year student.
- Word limits require students to be selective in their response to a task, demonstrating their judgement regarding the most important aspects of a topic.
- Word limits require students to avoid redundancy (repetition of information or unnecessary repetition of words).
- Word limits require students to write concisely, to avoid 'wordiness'.

Most universities allow you a 10 per cent leeway either side (this is what 'plus or minus 10 per cent' means), so a 2,500 word assignment needs to be between 2,250 (2,500 – 250) and 2,750 (2,500 + 250) words. One side of A4, typed in a standard font (say Arial 12pt) and using double line spacing, normally contains between 250 and 300 words; so you can get a rough idea of how many words you have got by multiplying the number of pages by this figure. For example, if you have typed 11 pages, you will have around 2,750–3,300 words in total. The word count usually excludes your reference list, but double-check with the module leader if this is not mentioned in the assessment guidelines.

Are you clear about the submission process?

Checklist

CROSS REFERENCE

Presentation

- Are you required to submit a hard copy or to upload your document via your VLE? (You may need to do both.)
- If submitting a hard copy, how many copies do you need to submit, and in what form (eg A4, printed on one side or on both sides, secured in a folder or stapled)?
- Do you need to complete and attach a **standard cover sheet**? Or are you expected to create your own cover sheet? (You may be able to do both.)
- Where do you need to hand in hard copies (eg the school office, the office of a particular member of staff)?
- If submitting online, do you know the exact procedure? Make sure you find out about this in good time. Perhaps ask the module lecturer if it is possible to do a practice submission beforehand. (Many lecturers arrange an unassessed

formative assignment and practice submission early in the course, so make sure you take advantage of such an opportunity.)

- Are you required to make your submission anonymous? (This is usually the case.) If so, have you been careful to make sure your name is not visible? Have you included your student number?

- Ensure you know the *exact* deadline for submission (including any personal deadlines or extensions you may have been given); electronic systems may deny a submission, or flag it up as late, at 4:01pm if the deadline is 4:00pm.

Editing and proofreading your final text

Before you hand in the final version of your text, you need to read through it with two separate aims in mind. The first type of reading should be a type of **final editing**, where you focus on meaning and flow, making sure that everything hangs together and makes sense. The second type of reading is **proofreading**, where you check the text for surface errors in spelling, grammar and punctuation. This is also an opportunity to pick up on any problems with typing or formatting. Many students overlook the first type of reading (a final edit of content, organisation and meaning), and focus purely on looking for mistakes. However, it is important to do both. The two processes will obviously overlap: while reading to check meaning, you might also catch a few mistakes; while proofreading, you might encounter a possible ambiguity, for instance. This is to be expected, but you should take care not to be distracted from your principal aim.

Editing your final text

Make sure you leave enough time to read through your work several times to ensure that another person reading your essay will be able to follow what you have said and understand the points you want to make.

Top tips

The final edit

- Reading out loud can help you put yourself in the reader's shoes and get a good sense of the flow and naturalness of the text.

- Trying to read the same text over and over is difficult to do, as your brain tends to switch off. Read it once, then put the text aside and go for a walk or make a cup of tea. You will come back to the text with fresh eyes.

CROSS REFERENCE

Chapter 2, Coherent texts and arguments, Editing and redrafting for coherence

Systematic treatment of names and titles

In social work, you will often be required to refer to the titles of professional organisations, such as the Health and Care Professions Council (HCPC), Local Authorities, the National Health Service, the Department for Education and the Department of Health. When referring to these, it is important to follow the conventions regarding the use of **capitalisation**, and as such note that the titles of organisations are capitalised, eg the Heath Care Professions Council and the National Health Service.

Many organisations are also known by their **acronyms**. An acronym is the short form of a multi-word name, usually formed using the first letter of each word, eg:

- Health and Care Professions Council (HCPC);
- the Department for Education (DfE);
- the National Health Service (NHS);
- the Department of Health (DH).

Often, people are more familiar with the acronym than the name, sometimes to the extent that they can be a little hazy on what it actually stands for!

In your writing, it is important to be systematic in your use of names and acronyms. The rule in academic writing is very simple: when you mention a term for the first time, you should use the full name, with the acronym following immediately in parentheses; after this, you should always use the acronym. The following example demonstrates this clearly.

> In 2012 the Health and Care Professions Council (HCPC) became the regulator for social work. In order to practice social work in England, social workers need to ensure they are named on the HCPC register.

CROSS
REFERENCE

Chapter 2,
Coherent
texts and
arguments

Systematic use of names and acronyms adds to the flow and coherence of the text.

Note that acronyms are different from **abbreviations**, which are formed by shortening a word, eg:

- approx (approximately);
- etc (from the Latin 'et cetera', meaning 'and so on').

The fact that something has been abbreviated is often indicated by the full stop at the end (approx., etc.), but this is often omitted (as in this book, for example). The important thing is to be consistent.

Systems for highlighting language

In academic writing, **bold**, *italics* and 'quotation marks' are often used to highlight text in some way. It is important that you are systematic and consistent in your use of these.

Task

Systems for highlighting language

What 'systems' for highlighting language are used by the writers below?

A

Obsessive Compulsive Disorder (OCD) is a common mental health disorder with two main parts. "Obsessions" are unwelcome thoughts or images that repeatedly appear. "Compulsions" are rituals which people feel compelled to repeat. OCD is derived from the Latin word obsidere which denotes being taken into possession or being pre-occupied.

B

Research into schizophrenia has often focused on the role of the family. In the 1950s, the focus appeared to be on the family's role in the *causation* of the disorder. Consider, for example, Lidz et al's notion of 'pathological' families (1965) and the 'double-bind' hypothesis of Bateson et al (1956).

C

Some behaviours that can enhance the therapeutic relationship use elements of both verbal and non-verbal communication. These include the skill of **active listening**. Active listening …

(Pryjmachuk, 2011, p 63)

Discussion: systems for highlighting language

- In A, the text uses italics for Latin terms, and double quotation marks for highlighting words whose meaning is being discussed.

- In B, the text uses italics for emphasis, and single quotation marks to quote terms from the literature. It is a good idea to reserve one type of quotation mark (single or double) for quotations only; this may be specified in your assessment guidelines, but, if not, just make sure you are consistent.

- In C, the text uses bold for the first mention of a key term. This is very common in textbooks as it helps students to identify important concepts.

Proofreading

Proofreading is the final component of the writing process. It is the process whereby you check the text for surface errors in spelling, grammar and punctuation, and make sure that there are no typing mistakes ('typos') or formatting errors/inconsistencies.

Proofreading is actually a thorny issue. Firstly, students sometimes confuse it with the editing and redrafting process described in Chapter 2 (including the 'final edit' referred to above). In fact, proofreading should only involve the correction of small surface errors; it should not involve changing the meaning or structure of your work.

Secondly, proofreading can be something you do yourself, or it can be something you ask or employ someone else to do. There are no uniform guidelines across UK universities with respect to this process, so it is important that you consider the issues involved carefully. If you decide to employ a professional proofreader, you should first find out if your university offers a proofreading service. If no official services are available, you should seek recommendations from friends or fellow students. When you have made a decision, make sure that you and the proofreader make contact beforehand to discuss the terms of your 'contract'.

You should both be very clear on what can be expected. The proofreader can be asked to clean up surface errors in spelling, grammar and punctuation, but they should not be involved in changing the structure or meaning of your work. There are good reasons for this: firstly, universities obviously expect work submitted by students to be their own work in essence (though they accept that students may ask for help with grammar and punctuation); secondly, you do not want your own voice or message to be distorted in any way.

Thirdly, be very clear that anyone who proofreads your work is merely *making suggestions*; it is then up to you to consider these, and to accept or reject them. Ultimately, only you are responsible for your work.

Top tips

Proofreading

- Become adept at proofreading your own writing by noting the kind of errors that have been picked up on in previous assignments, and focusing on these.

- Make use of the spelling and grammar check tool of your word processing program. Microsoft Word will indicate spelling mistakes by underlining them in red, and grammar mistakes by underlining them in green. (These will also help you identify some typing and formatting issues, eg, too many/no spaces between words.) This is a very useful tool, but it is to be treated with caution: it is a computer program, not a human being, and thus, sometimes cannot identify a particular nuance in a text. You need to assess each suggestion carefully.

- You should always be involved in proofreading your own work, but many people, including experienced academics, sometimes ask a peer or colleague to look at their writing. In this way, proofreading can become a type of collaborative activity, one that could enable you to develop a skill that will be essential in future academic studies and your work life. This is distinct from the academic malpractice of collusion, where a student takes credit for work they are not responsible for.

Task

Proofreading practice

 Find and correct errors of spelling, grammar, punctuation and formatting in the following texts.

A

Social workers have a generic knowledge and skilled base. Traditionally, Ba Social Work programme have lasted 3 years and Ma 2 years, however, there are now alternative routes to qualification. Social Work can now qualify via fast track or the higher apprenticeships programmes.

B

Of central importance, to the cognitive psychologists is the 'schema' notion. A schema is a mental "template" that guides behaviour or thought, in a similar way that a recipe is a template for creating an exotic dish [schemata actually guide external and external action, external action being observable behaviour, internal action being thought]. Any action, internal or external, will have a schema underpinning it.

Thus, there are schemata for skilled tasks, like driving or typing, schemata for making judgements about people, schemata for language, schemata for perceiving, and so on. some aspect's of certain schemata may be inherited (indeed, the simplest schemata are mere reflex action's), the vast majority are acquired. To those familiar with Computers, a schema is little more than the software that drives our action. however, unlike Computer Software, schemata can replicate,change and become redundant as we experience the world.

Schemata, help us process the vast amount, of information in the world. they serve us well for the majority of the time; however, they are not always applicable to a particular situation and when we misapply them, error's occur, for example, when we misapply a "braking" schema whilst driving,we might be involved in an accident. Similarly,the misapplication of 'judgemental' schemata can lead to the creation of stereotypes.

Formatting

In written assessments, you will be judged on the breadth of your knowledge, the depth of your understanding, the quality of your ideas and analysis, and the clarity and coherence of your writing. However, even the best work cannot fully impress the reader if it is poorly formatted and presented. Untidy presentation and inconsistent formatting will hinder the reader's ability to navigate your text. It can also suggest a 'sloppy' or unprofessional approach. It is for these reasons that formatting and presentation usually form part of the criteria for assessment in marking descriptors.

CROSS REFERENCE

Studying for your Social Work Degree, Chapter 6, Assessment

The following tasks will help you understand how seemingly minor formatting choices can greatly affect the reader. The subsequent discussions will guide you towards formatting and presenting your work clearly and professionally.

Line spacing

Task

Line spacing

Look at the three versions of work below. What differences do you notice in the formatting of the text? Which version is usually *not* acceptable in university work? Why?

A

Social media is a relatively new phenomenon. Ten years ago Twitter, Facebook, YouTube, Pinterest, Flickr!, Linkedin, and other social media applications were at best a twinkle in somebody's eye. Words like 'app' had not entered our vocabulary. Mobile phones were no longer 'bricks', but had not yet become smart. As social media applications began to emerge, interest grew in how social media might support practice-based learning (Thackray et al, 2007; Scantlebury, 2008; Dunworth and Scantlebury, 2006; Scantlebury et al, 2008; Waldman and Rafferty, 2008).

B

Social media is a relatively new phenomenon. Ten years ago Twitter, Facebook, YouTube, Pinterest, Flickr!, Linkedin, and other social media applications were at best a twinkle in somebody's eye. Words like 'app' had not entered our vocabulary. Mobile phones were no longer 'bricks', but had not yet become smart. As social media applications began to emerge, interest grew in how social media might support practice-based learning (Thackray et al, 2007; Scantlebury, 2008; Dunworth and Scantlebury, 2006; Scantlebury et al, 2008; Waldman and Rafferty, 2008).

C

Social media is a relatively new phenomenon. Ten years ago Twitter, Facebook, YouTube, Pinterest, Flickr!, Linkedin, and other social media applications were at best a twinkle in somebody's eye. Words like 'app' had not entered our vocabulary. Mobile phones were no longer 'bricks', but had not yet become smart. As social media applications began to emerge, interest grew in how social media might support practice-based learning (Thackray et al, 2007; Scantlebury, 2008; Dunworth and Scantlebury, 2006; Scantlebury et al, 2008; Waldman and Rafferty, 2008).

Discussion: line spacing

The three texts have been formatted with different line spacing. A is **single-spaced**, B is **1.5 spaced**, and C is **double-spaced**. (In Microsoft Word, line spacing is adjusted through the 'paragraph' tool on the toolbar.) Assessment guidelines usually specify the line spacing you should use. Most guidelines specify 1.5 or double spaced, for two reasons.

- Most people find single-spaced writing a bit difficult to read.
- The person assessing your work may wish to add comments or corrections directly onto the text, either on paper, or using VLE tools such as Feedback Studio (Blackboard) and this is not possible when the line spacing is too narrow.

Paragraph formatting

Task

Paragraph formatting

Look at the four versions of work below. What differences do you notice in the formatting of paragraphs? Which version is *not* acceptable? Why?

A

The family has played a central role in research into schizophrenia since the 1950s when, admittedly, the focus appeared to be on the family's role in the causation of the disorder. Consider, for example, Lidz et al's notion of 'pathological' families (1965) and the 'double-bind' hypothesis of Bateson et al (1956).
Around the same time as these 'causal' hypotheses were being promoted, the anti-psychotic drugs were discovered. Drugs, by their very nature, are treatments designated for the individual and this fact coupled with the prevailing view of families as toxic agents led, unsurprisingly, to what could cynically be called the first family intervention strategy – that of excluding the family.

B

The family has played a central role in research into schizophrenia since the 1950s when, admittedly, the focus appeared to be on the family's role in the causation of the disorder. Consider, for example, Lidz et al's notion of 'pathological' families (1965) and the 'double-bind' hypothesis of Bateson et al (1956).

Around the same time as these 'causal' hypotheses were being promoted, the anti-psychotic drugs were discovered. Drugs, by their very nature, are treatments designated for the individual and this fact coupled with the prevailing view of families as toxic agents led, unsurprisingly, to what could cynically be called the first family intervention strategy – that of excluding the family.

C

    The family has played a central role in research into schizophrenia since the 1950s when, admittedly, the focus appeared to be on the family's role in the causation of the disorder. Consider, for example, Lidz et al's notion of 'pathological' families (1965) and the 'double-bind' hypothesis of Bateson et al (1956).
    Around the same time as these 'causal' hypotheses were being promoted, the anti-psychotic drugs were discovered. Drugs, by their very nature, are treatments designated for the individual and this fact coupled with the prevailing view of families as toxic agents led, unsurprisingly, to what could cynically be called the first family intervention strategy – that of excluding the family.

▲ **D**

The family has played a central role in research into schizophrenia since the 1950s when, admittedly, the focus appeared to be on the family's role in the causation of the disorder. Consider, for example, Lidz et al's notion of 'pathological' families (1965) and the 'double-bind' hypothesis of Bateson et al (1956).

Around the same time as these 'causal' hypotheses were being promoted, the anti-psychotic drugs were discovered. Drugs, by their very nature, are treatments designated for the individual and this fact coupled with the prevailing view of families as toxic agents led, unsurprisingly, to what could cynically be called the first family intervention strategy – that of excluding the family.

CROSS
REFERENCE

Chapter 2,
Coherent
texts and
arguments,
Cohesion and
paragraph
structure

Discussion: paragraph formatting

Most people find A difficult to read because the paragraphs are not clearly distinguished. B, C and D distinguish paragraphs in different ways: B has a line space between paragraphs; C starts each paragraph with an indentation. D uses both a line space and indentation. If there is indentation, the line space is not strictly necessary, but it does serve to make the distinction between paragraphs even clearer. It is very important that paragraphs are clearly distinguished. This ties in with the discussion in Chapter 2, where you saw how 'cohesive' paragraphs deal with a single, unified idea. Your formatting should underline this sense of cohesion.

Formatting tables and diagrams

It is important that tables and diagrams are labelled clearly and consistently. The examples below show the typical convention in academic writing, ie tables are labelled at the top, and diagrams are labelled at the bottom. If tables and diagrams are taken or adapted from other sources, they should be clearly referenced. The use of **bold** in labels should follow assessment guidelines; if this is not specified, just make sure you are consistent.

Example of a table:

Table 1: Treatments for depression according to patient group

GROUP	TREATMENT
1	Antidepressants
2	Problem-solving
3	Cognitive behavioural therapy
4	Physical exercise

Example of a figure:

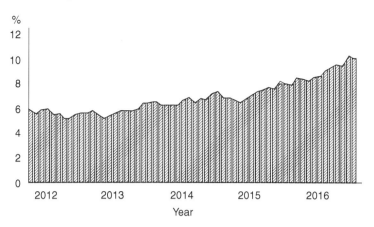

Figure 2: Percentage of social work students in paid employment over the academic holidays

If you have included tables and figures, make sure that you have referred to them clearly in the text, eg:

- As Table 1 shows/illustrates, …

- As can be seen in Table 1, …

- Figure 2 shows/illustrates …

- The RDA increases according to age (Table 1).

- The number of students entering paid employment continues to rise (Figure 2).

Presentation

First impressions are important. The way your assignment looks says a lot about your approach to your studies. A well-presented piece of work shows that you are professional, pay attention to detail, and care about your work. It signals respect for the people who have set and will mark the assessment. It is not about decorating your work or making it striking to look at; it is about creating a document which is professional, clear and easy to navigate.

What should my essay look like?

1) It should have a title page

This should be the first sheet. Even if you are required to use a standard cover sheet for your assignments, there is no reason why you cannot also have a title page. You may be provided with guidelines on what to include, but if not, you may wish to include some or all of the following:

- your name (or your Student ID Number if the assignment is to be submitted anonymously, which it nearly always is nowadays);

- the institution for which it is being submitted, eg 'University of Towncaster – School of Social Work and Nursing';
- the title of the assignment;
- the course/module/programme for which it was written (including the date you commenced the course);
- the date of submission or the date you completed the assessment;
- your course unit leader's name and/or your academic adviser's name.

An example is given below:

The University of Towncaster
School of Social Work and Nursing

BSWK (Hons)

(2017 Cohort)

SWK17727 Learning for Professional Practice

Reflective Essay

Student: 0012345

Submission date: 6th October 2017

Course Unit Lead: Dr C Lead

Academic Adviser: Dr A Adviser

---

2) The word count should be written on the document

Make it very clear that you have met the word limit by writing the word count at the end of the document. In Microsoft Word, the word count of a document is clearly visible in the bottom left-hand corner of the screen.

3) Your pages should be numbered

If you or a lecturer prints out copies, it is very easy to get things in the wrong order if the pages are not secured together. In Microsoft Word, page numbers are added using the 'insert' tool on the toolbar. You can format these in a number of ways (eg bottom of the page, top of the page, centred, right-hand corner, left-hand corner). Experiment until you find a style that suits you, or that works well with a particular document.

4) It should be written using an appropriate font

Academic work should be written in a font which is easy to read and appropriately 'serious'. This may be specified in the guidelines. If not, use either:

- Times New Roman
- Arial

Inappropriate fonts include:

- *Comic Sans*

Comic Sans is a popular, 'friendly' font, but it tends to make documents look childish (which explains why it is used in many primary schools).

In Microsoft Word, font (and size – see below) can be easily selected from the toolbar.

5) The font size should be readable and appropriate

Don't use too large or too small a font size. A font size of 12pt is ideal; anything above font size 14pt will appear rather childish, and anything below 10pt will be far too small to read comfortably. Larger font sizes may be used for headings and subheadings. Again, this may be specified in the assessment guidelines.

6) It should look professional

Do not decorate your scripts with fancy pictures and colours. Aim for a professional look, rather than a decorative or striking one.

7) It should follow printing guidelines

Many universities now require you to submit your written assessments electronically, but on those occasions when you are required to print out hard copies, check guidelines on whether you should print on both sides or on one side only. You will often need to print out hard copies of documents for your **portfolio**.

And finally ...

Finding advice and support

Universities provide a range of academic writing support. This goes by different names, including 'insessional classes', 'academic literacy support' and 'study skills', and will cover academic writing and other skills, such as speaking or critical thinking. The provision may distinguish between home students and international students, or it may be aimed at both sets of students. This type of integrated provision is becoming more common as it has been recognised that the most problematic issues in academic writing, such as coherence and style, affect all students, not just international students. Of course, students who speak English as a second language may also need specific English-language support, and many universities offer classes in areas such as grammar and pronunciation.

As well as academic writing classes, most universities have 'writing consultations', sometimes known as 'writing tutorials'. These involve meeting with an expert in English language and academic skills to discuss a piece of your writing. The length of these consultations varies, but they usually range from 30 minutes to an hour. You are usually required to send the work in advance. This could be an assignment for which you have already received a mark and feedback, or an assignment which you are currently working on. In the former case, the tutor will be able to help you understand why you received the mark and the feedback you did. In the latter case, the tutor will be able to give you advice on how to improve the piece of work before submission. In both cases, the real focus is not on that particular piece of work, but on you as a developing academic writer: it is a formative consultation rather than a proofreading service. The tutor may help you to correct some errors of grammar, punctuation and style, but they are more likely to focus on issues of clarity, coherence, style and readability. The advice you receive should help you develop your academic writing skills and apply these to future work. The fact that the tutor is very unlikely to be an expert in social work is actually an advantage, as it will provide a test of whether your explanations of concepts and theories are accessible to a non-expert, as they should be. If you do want help with a piece of work in progress, make sure you leave enough time before submission, as it can take a few weeks to go through the university's booking system.

Summary

This chapter has guided you through the process of preparing your work for submission so as to meet the expectations of your lecturers at university. It has advised you on how to approach the final editing and proofreading process, and it has discussed the issues surrounding proofreading. It has provided you with information and guidance on formatting and presentation, and a presentation 'checklist' that you can apply to any piece of work before submitting it. Finally, it has offered advice on what you can do if you feel you need further professional support with your writing. You should now be ready to submit your writing for assessment, confident in the knowledge that you have done all you can to meet the expectations of your lecturers.

Sources of example texts

Ayhan, H, Iyigun, E, Ince, S, Can, M, Hatipoglu, S and Saglam, M (2015) A Randomised Clinical Trial Comparing the Patient Comfort and Efficacy of Three Different Graduated Compression Stockings in the Prevention of Postoperative Deep Vein Thrombosis. *Journal of Clinical Nursing*, 24, 2247–57.

Pryjmachuk, S (2011) The Capable Mental Health Nurse. In Pryjmachuk, S (ed) *Mental Health Nursing: An Evidence-Based Introduction*. London: Sage, 42–72.

Thackray, L. (2014) Obstacles to Engagement with Social Media. In Westwood, J. (Ed) *Social Media in Social Work Education*. St. Albans: Critical Publishing.

Triggle, N (2017) NHS Operations: Waiting Times to Rise in 'Trade-off', Boss Says. *BBC News*, 31st March [online]. Available at: www.bbc.co.uk/news/health-39420662 (accessed 2 April 2017).

Appendix 1
English language references

This is not meant to be an exhaustive list of resources, but rather a selection of those that we think you may find most useful.

Dictionaries

There are many online dictionaries, but if you prefer to feel the weight of one in your hands, then Chambers is a good choice:

Chambers 21st Century Dictionary (1999) Edinburgh: Chambers Harrap Publishers Ltd.

A good online dictionary, especially for students whose first language is not English, is the Cambridge Dictionary. The definitions are very clear and easy to understand, and there is an excellent pronunciation tool:

Cambridge Dictionary [online]. Available at: http://dictionary.cambridge.org/ (accessed 26 March 2017).

Grammar books

Caplan, N (2012) *Grammar Choices for Graduate and Professional Writers*. Ann Arbor, MI: University of Michigan Press.

Caplan's book is aimed at postgraduate students (known as 'graduate' students in the USA, where this book is published). Nevertheless, if you are looking for a systematic analysis of English grammar in the context of academic English, you may find this book very useful. It contains many clear examples of grammar in use in real-life academic writing.

Hewings, M (2015) *Advanced Grammar in Use*. 3rd ed. Cambridge: Cambridge University Press.

Murphy, R (2015) *English Grammar in Use*. 4th ed. Cambridge: Cambridge University Press.

Murphy, R (2015) *Essential Grammar in Use*. 4th ed. Cambridge: Cambridge University Press.

The Grammar in Use series is particularly useful for students whose first language is not English. The books present each grammar point in a clear and systematic way, and provide exercises and a self-study answer key. There are also lots of multimedia features in recent editions.

Other resources

Academic Phrasebank. [online] Available at: www.phrasebank.manchester.ac.uk/ (accessed 14 May 2017).

Academic Word List. [online] Available at: www.victoria.ac.nz/lals/resources/ academicwordlist (accessed 2 April 2017).

Baily, S (2011) *Academic Writing for International Students of English*. 3rd ed. Oxon: Routledge.

Bottomley, J (2014) *Academic Writing for International Students of Science*. Oxon: Routledge.

Peck, J and Cole, M (2012) *Write it Right: The Secrets of Effective Writing*. 2nd ed. New York: Palgrave Macmillan.

Swales, J and Feak, C (2012) *Academic Writing for Graduate Students: Essential Tasks and Skills*. 3rd ed. Michigan: Michigan ELT.

Appendix 2
Grammatical terminology

GRAMMATICAL TERM	DEFINITION	EXAMPLES
adjective	a word which describes a **noun**	an <u>elderly</u> woman a <u>comprehensive</u> test
adverb	a word which adds information to a **verb** or an **adjective**	attend a <u>weekly</u> support group a <u>very</u> long report
article	the words 'a/an' and 'the', used with **nouns**	<u>a</u> desk <u>the</u> multi-disciplinary team
clause	a structure containing a **verb**, forming a sentence, or joining with other clauses to form sentences	(1) <u>This essay aims to explore current interventions in social work practice.</u> (1) <u>The young woman could not attend the meeting</u> (2) <u>because there was no public transport</u>. (1) <u>Founded in 1898</u>, (2) <u>the charity has long provided support for the local community</u>.
conjunction (linking word/phrase)	a word or phrase that joins words, phrases or **clauses**	service users <u>and</u> carers take once a day <u>but</u> only after a meal The <u>young woman</u> could not attend the meeting (main clause) <u>because</u> there was no public transport (subordinate clause). <u>If</u> your depression persists (subordinate clause), an appointment with your GP may be required (main clause).
contraction	two words joined by an apostrophe	<u>he's</u> a good father <u>it's</u> 4pm
countable noun*	a **noun** which can be counted and so can be used in the **plural**	a <u>social worker</u>, <u>social workers</u> the <u>service user</u>, <u>service users</u>

GRAMMATICAL TERM	DEFINITION	EXAMPLES
main clause	the **clause** containing the main idea in a **sentence**	This essay aims to explore current interventions in social work practice. The young woman could not attend the meeting because there was no public transport. Founded in 1898, the charity has long provided support for the local community. The study suggests that this is a promising way of supporting independence.
noun	people, places or things	child, adult, home, training
participle clause	a **clause** with an '–ing' or '–ed' verb form adding information to the **main clause**	Founded in 1898, the charity has long provided support for the local community. The study investigated the effects of chronic illness on families, using mixed methods research.
plural	the form of a **noun** that refers to more than one, usually ending in 's' in English	social workers, babies, women, men, children, criteria (irregular plurals)
possessive	a word or phrase which denotes belonging	her child Mrs Brown's child the child is hers
proper noun	a noun written with a capital letter, as it is the name of a person, place, company etc	Manchester, HCPC, Tavistock Clinic, CMHT
sentence	a group of words usually beginning with a capital letter and ending in a full stop, and containing a **subject** and a **verb**; the main building blocks of writing	Students are advised to make an appointment with their academic adviser. This essay aims to explore current interventions in social work practice. The young woman could not attend the review meeting because there was no public transport. Founded in 1823, the hospital has long provided health care for the local community. The study suggests that this is a promising treatment.

GRAMMATICAL TERM	DEFINITION	EXAMPLES
singular	the form of a **noun** that refers to one of something	a home the social worker
subject	the person or thing which the **verb** relates to and agrees with in number	<u>Students</u> are advised to make an appointment with their academic adviser. <u>The study</u> suggests that this is a promising way of supporting independence.
that-clause	a **subject/verb** structure that follows certain verbs etc that are usually followed by 'that'	The study suggests <u>that this is a promising way of supporting independence</u>.
uncountable noun*	a **noun** seen as a mass which cannot be split or counted, and so cannot be **plural**	pain, time, energy, cancer
quantifier	a word or phrase which denotes 'how much' of a **noun**	<u>few</u> people <u>a large amount of</u> money
verb	a word expressing an action or state	be, have, go, wash, eat, love Students <u>are</u> advised to make an appointment with their academic adviser. The study <u>suggests</u> that this is a promising way of supporting independence.

*This is often about how a noun is interpreted in a particular context, rather than an absolute concept. Many nouns can be countable or uncountable depending on the context, eg:

research into **cancer**

many **cancers** can be treated with chemotherapy

nurses can administer **medicine**

a new **medicine**

Appendix 3
Key phrases in assignments

PHRASE	LEVEL	MEANING
analyse	Mostly Levels 5 and 6, especially with the word 'critically'; rarely Level 4	Look at the concepts and ideas under discussion in depth; the addition of 'critically' means look at the concepts and ideas in depth **and** with a critical eye
assess	All levels, though common at lower levels	Make comments about the value/importance of the concepts and ideas under discussion
compare	All levels, though common at lower levels	Look for similarities between the concepts and ideas under discussion
contrast	All levels, though common at lower levels	Look for differences between the concepts and ideas under discussion; often used with 'compare' (see above)
define	All levels, though common at lower levels	State precisely what is meant by a particular issue, theory or concept
discuss	Level 5 and above; sometimes Level 4	Give reasons for and against; investigate and examine by argument
evaluate	Mostly Levels 5 and 6, especially with the word 'critically'	Weigh up the arguments surrounding an issue, using your own opinions and, more importantly, reference to the work of others
illustrate	All levels	Make clear by the use of examples
outline	All levels, though tends to be used with the lower levels	Give the main features of
review	All levels, though 'critically review' would imply Level 5 and above	Extract relevant information from a document or set of documents
state	All levels, though tends to be used with the lower levels	Present in a clear, concise form

PHRASE	LEVEL	MEANING
summarise	All levels, though tends to be used with the lower levels	Give an account of all the main points of the concepts and ideas under discussion
with reference to	All levels	Use a specific context, issue or concept to make the meaning clear

Appendix 4
Academic levels at university

UNDERGRADUATE STUDY			
ENGLAND, WALES, NORTHERN IRELAND	**SCOTLAND**	**AWARD**	**NOTES**
Level 4	Level 7	Certificate of Higher Education (CertHE)	
Level 5	Level 8	Diploma of Higher Education (DipHE) Foundation Degree (FdD)	Up until 2009, minimum academic qualification for social workers
Level 6	Level 9	Ordinary Bachelor Degree	Minimum academic qualification for social workers
	Level 10	Bachelor Degree with Honours	Usual academic qualification for social workers
POSTGRADUATE STUDY			
Level 7	Level 11	Masters Degree, eg MSc, MA, MPhil Postgraduate Certificate or Diploma (PGCert; PGDip)	Common qualification for social workers who had a first degree
Level 8	Level 12	Research Doctorate (PhD) Professional Doctorate	Becoming more common in the profession

Answer key

Chapter 1
Reflective essays, Task (pages 23–24)

A   Description of a situation and feelings

B   Analysis of feelings

C/D Action taken at the time, exploration of the issues, resulting outcomes, understanding achieved, future action identified

Chapter 2
Organisational frameworks, Task (pages 33–36)

1)

A Classification: factors affecting a young child's development, exemplification

B Classification: 1) how we communicate, 2) who we communicate to

C Problem-solution: ways of tackling alcohol misuse

D Classification: responses to HIV diagnosis – perhaps chronological stages

E Cause-effect (reasons for rise in earnings) and problem-solution

F Compares and contrasts alternative viewpoints in the literature

2)

A

Introduction/background – refer to title

- Definition of 'outcomes' and 'young care leavers'
- Factors influencing (presence or absence of support networks; whether in education or employment, physical and mental health (current and past); whether there is evidence of resilience; diet, environment, lifestyle, socio-economic status, cultural factors)
- Extent to which social workers can influence
- compare with influence of others, eg foster parents, teachers

Conclusion – social workers can have an impact, but other factors influencing outcomes (listed above) have more – potential of social workers to influence other factors

B

Introduction/background – claimed that communication is the <u>core</u> skill of social work

- Definition of communication
- Different types of communication: verbal, written, non-verbal
- Different forms of communication: service users and carers, colleagues, other professional organisations

- Relative importance of (other) different core skills, eg problem solving skills, organisational skills, prioritising workload, having good time management – less important than communication?
- How communication impacts on other aspects of social work – thus more important?
- Problems caused by breakdown in communication (eg as noted in Serious Case Reviews)

Conclusion – social workers need a range of skills but communication is integral to all, and very difficult to be a good social worker without good communication skills, even if competent in other core skills

General and specific information, Task (page 43)

General: What must you consider in relation to your conduct as a professional and a member of a professional body?

It is important not only to consider your conduct while in work; you must also remember that as a professional and a member of a professional body, you are under scrutiny at all times.

Specific: issue/problem

Think about when you go out with your friends on a Saturday night ... you MUST consider who may see you, what you are doing and that you are still representing the organisation you work for.

Specific: consequence and what it means for you as a social worker

Unfortunately you are never really off duty in that you are always answerable for your actions.

Old and new information, Task (page 44)

Phrases in **bold** refer back to information underlined

Patients and service users are being encouraged to take more control of their own care (Department of Health, 2009) and they have an important part to play in determining how services are designed, implemented and evaluated (The Kings Fund, 2012). By collaborating with service users and responding appropriately to their feedback, social workers, nurses and other healthcare staff can deliver more appropriate care and ensure that any concerns raised are dealt with quickly and appropriately (Coulter, 2012). **This** will usually involve collecting and using information provided by patients (eg patient satisfaction surveys or focus groups) in order to deliver the kind of services that patients want. **Whichever approach** is used, the key aim is to find out what patients really think about the services we provide and provide supporting evidence of **this**.

Noun or pronoun?, Task (pages 45–46)

Fatigue is commonly experienced by people suffering from a variety of chronic illnesses. In the sixteenth century, the concept of fatigue was related to a tedious duty; nowadays, fatigue is understood as a state of feeling tired for 'no reason'; Barsevick et al (2010) define it as a subjective state, a feeling unrelated to that of being tired after exercise or relieved after rest. It may be regarded as exhaustive, unpredictable in its course, and affecting cognitive ability. Fatigue is often described as multidimensional and disabling, affecting the quality of life of those living with it. It is associated with negative emotions such as anxiety, numbness and vulnerability. These are likely to impact on social relationships and family life, often leading to withdrawal and social isolation.

Notes

Other combinations are possible; the important thing to remember is to avoid ambiguity and to be sensitive to the reader's need to be reminded of the topic frequently.

Referring back in the text to summarise and comment, Task (pages 47–48)

1)

a) approach

b) population

c) approach

d) This, analysis

e) case

f) research

2)

a) family support

b) these Acts (could also be 'this legislation')

c) these findings

d) This ability to self-govern our behaviours

Linking ideas, Task (pages 51–52)

1)

a) In addition (it is an additional point, but not a more important one)

b) In contrast ('on the contrary' contradicts a negative or a question, eg 'He is not fit to work. On the contrary, he has a serious condition which requires total rest.'

c) albeit (has the same meaning as 'although' but is used before noun/adjective/ adverb phrases, not subjects and verbs)

d) whereby ('a process whereby' is a common phrase)

e) thereby (usually followed by -ing; 'hereby' is usually only used in very formal phrases such as 'I hereby pronounce you …')

f) namely ('in other words', precedes an explanation of what has just been said)

g) respectively (refers back to two things in the same order)

h) the former, the latter (very useful for referring back precisely)

2)

Feelings of anxiety are experienced by everyone at some point in our lives. ~~Furthermore,~~ some people have a specific cause for their anxious feelings, for example if they have divorced, been recently bereaved or moved house. Other people cannot identify a specific trigger for their feelings of anxiety. ~~However, given that~~ when we are anxious everyone experiences similar symptoms, even though they may vary in intensity and frequency. ~~While~~ avoiding situations that make us anxious can provide short-term relief, avoidance is not the best long-term coping strategy as the anxiety returns when we are represented with the trigger situation.

Chapter 3
Referencing errors, Task (pages 71–72)

1)

a) There is no publication year, which name-year (Harvard) systems require:

> According to Tarrier and Barrowclough (1996), carers need information, and professionals have a moral duty to supply it.

b) This citation is information-prominent. Both the name and the date should be in brackets, and at the end of the sentence and before the full stop:

> The major hindrance appears to be the cultural dominance of 'technical rationality' (Schön, 1988).

c) Alphabetical sequencing is required to distinguish between two publications in the same year:

> In a theoretical paper, Dickoff and James (1968a) argue this position, which is subsequently backed up by a further, data-based paper (Dickoff and James, 1968b).

d) Round, rather than square, brackets are the norm:

> Meleis (2001) speculates that historical and cultural paternalism are largely to blame.

e) This citation is a direct quote so the quote must be enclosed in speech marks and the page number must be provided. Since it's a quote that actively involves the author's name, the year needs to be in brackets:

> To quote from Benner (1984): 'Expertise develops when the clinician tests and refines propositions, hypotheses and principle-based expectations in actual practice situations' (p 37).

Alternatively:

> To quote from Benner (1984, p 37): 'Expertise develops when the clinician tests and refines propositions, hypotheses and principle-based expectations in actual practice situations.'

f) The authors' initials are not required in the main body of text* (only the final reference list):

> According to Green (2008) women are the primary carers in society.
> * There is an exception when you have authors with the same surname who have published in the same year and you want to distinguish between them in your work. For example, if you had used a book by Mary Green from 2008 and also one by Helen Green from 2008, you'd refer to the first as M Green (2008) and the second as H Green (2008).

g) With two or more authors, you use 'et al' in the main body of text (but list all authors in the final reference list):

> The results are consistent with the findings of Posner et al (2012).

h) Round brackets are required rather than square ones, and there is no year for Smith:

> Smith (1989, cited by Jones 1992) suggests that the findings are incomplete.

i) The following is more academic:

> … (see, for example, the 'change spiral' of Lewin, 1958).

j) The citation actively involves the author (is author-prominent) so the brackets need to go round the year only:

> Schon (1988) suggests that this paradox can be resolved by acknowledging the importance of subjectivity.

2)

Note that there may be slight variations in styles across publishers and departments.

a) Koprowska, J (2014) *Communication and Interpersonal Skills in Social Work*. Exeter: Learning Matters.

b) Lloyd, C, King, R, and Chenoweth, L (2002) Social Work, Stress and Burnout: A Review. *Journal of Mental Health*, 11(3), 255–65.

c) Payne, M (2014) *Modern Social Work Theory*. London: Palgrave Macmillan.

d) Matthias, M S, Salyers, M P, Rollins, A I and Frankel, R M (2012) Decision Making in Recovery-oriented Mental Health Care. *Psychiatric Rehabilitation Journal*, 35, 305–14.

e) Judd, R G and Johnston, L B (2012) Ethical Consequences of Using Social Network Sites for Students in Professional Social Work Programs. *Journal of Social Work Values and Ethics*, 9(1): 5–12.

f) Kinman, G and Grant, L (2011) Exploring Stress Resilience in Trainee Social Workers: The Role of Emotional and Social Competencies. *British Journal of Social Work*, 41, 261–75.

g) Social Exclusion Unit (2002) *Reducing Re-offending by Ex-prisoners*. London: Social Exclusion Unit.

h) Parsonage, M, Fossey, M and Tutty, C (2012) *Liaison Psychiatry in the Modern NHS*. London: Centre for Mental Health. Available at: www.centreformentalhealth. org.uk/liaison-psychiatry-nhs (accessed 14 May 2017).

Focus, Task (pages 76–78)

1)

Information-prominent: b, d, f

Author-prominent: a, c, e

2)

a) <u>As</u> Wright (1993) <u>points out</u>, one of the paradoxes of successful change is that it escapes public notice simply because it is successful.

c) <u>According to</u> Scheidlinger and Aronson (2001), group therapy has been used to treat a wide range of symptomolotalogy in adolescents.

e) Musson (2017) <u>argues that</u> psychodynamic theory can offer important insights to guide social work assessment and analysis.

3)

a) advocate

b) identify/identified

c) acknowledge

d) distinguishes between

e) argues that

f) defined

Chapter 4

Being concise, Task (page 84)

Square brackets, eg [the country of] = unnecessary

Strike through, eg ~~and learned about~~ = definitely needs to be deleted (completely redundant or 'tautological', or extremely wordy)

[It was] in 1864 [that] teacher and artist Octavia Hill (1838–1912) [first] started to work in the poorer neighbourhoods of late Victorian inner London (in what is now the borough of Marylebone, which is ~~in inner London and~~ nowadays ~~is~~ one of the most expensive places to live ~~in the capital~~). She worked with people at the bottom of the social ladder: the poor, unemployed, ~~those who couldn't find work~~, all living in cold and damp ~~London~~ dwellings. Housing was her main concern. Hill believed that a well maintained home, however small ~~or compact~~, with light, air and space – with neighbours who care about each other – is one of life's main necessities.

Notes

'It was' is not necessary

'first' is not required

'Marylebone in inner London' is redundant because we are told earlier in the same sentence that she was working in inner London.

'in the capital' repeats what has already been made clear in the article that Octavia Hill's work is taking place in London.

'those who couldn't find work' is a repetition of unemployed, so it's not necessary to include.

'London dwellings' London is not needed in this sentence as it is clear this is taking place in London.

'Small or compact' in this context either one will do but both are saying the same thing.

Being precise, Task (pages 84–85)

1) evolved

2) invasive

3) determine

4) exhibiting

5) administer

6) diagnostic

7) in terms of

8) associated with

Identifying inappropriate language, Task (pages 88–89)

1) male/man/~~bloke~~

2) inebriated/~~tipsy~~/drunk

3) ~~impecunious~~/poor/~~broke~~

4) food/nutrition/~~grub~~

5) sleep/~~slumber/doze~~

Identifying formal language, Task (page 89)

1) Little

2) deteriorated

3) was awarded

4) approximately

5) adhere

6) demonstrate

7) ensure

8) such as

9) improve

10) facilitate

11) An increasing number of

12) many

Improving style, Task (page 91)

The ageing population means that **an increasing number of** people have to be carers and **many** of them are struggling. They often **do not** receive help and **they are** facing cuts in the benefits and services they **are entitled to.** **A number of studies have reported that** the general well-being of carers **deteriorates** the more hours of carer they **provide**. A positive partnership with professionals will **greatly remove** outcomes for both carers and service users. All professionals, **including** social workers, doctors, district nurses **and** general practice nurses, should respect carers as expert partners in care. **Furthermore**, social workers need to have certain values and skills **such as** compassion, competence, commitment, to make sure carers' well-being is being looked after.

Commonly confused words, Task (page 94)

1) practice

2) practise

3) advice

4) advise

5) device

6) devised

7) licensed

8) licence

9) effects

10) affected

11) their

12) There

Variation in comma use, Task (page 99)

B separates phrases and clauses using commas; A does not. It is arguably easier for the reader to have these commas. A could have three commas:

The assessment of a person's capacity to give or withhold consent is considered in relation to a specific decision. While the individual may not have capacity to make some decisions, they may still retain capacity for other decisions. For example, a patient may not have capacity to make a decision regarding a surgical procedure, but could retain capacity to consent (or not) to having their clinical observations (eg blood pressure) checked.

Grammar and punctuation, Task (page 102)

1)

Social factors also seem to influence depression rates. Depression is more common in the unemployed, those living alone, those who are divorced or separated, those living in local authority or housing association accommodation, those with a lower socioeconomic status and/or material disadvantage, and those with no formal educational qualifications. Social factors such as isolation, racist attacks and dissatisfaction with housing may also contribute to depression in refugee groups. Indeed, in traumatised refugees and asylum seekers, poor social support seems to be a stronger predictor of depression in the long term than the severity of the initial trauma.

2)

Postnatal depression affects 10–15 in every 100 women after childbirth. It can be difficult to detect because it may present differently in different women. The symptoms of postnatal depression are similar to those of depression at any other stage of life; the difference is the presence of a baby, which is likely to be the focus of the woman's thoughts and difficulties. The disorder may be mild or severe. Milder forms might be treated within the primary healthcare team, while more severe forms will require additional input from psychiatric services. Diagnosing postnatal depression requires clinical assessment by a GP or mental health specialist. However, nursing and midwifery staff must be alert to the disorder in order make timely referrals.

Parallel structures, Task (page 104)

1)

Recording errors can impact on service users, social workers and organisations.

Or

Recording errors can impact on all stakeholders: patients, nurses and organisations.

2)

One initiative which aims to help young adults with a diagnosed mental health problem settle into accommodation is the Early Support and Intervention Programme. This programme aims to:

- help young people manage and keep their tenancies;
- improve young people's living skills, eg budgeting, home and self-care;
- support community integration;
- promote access to employment, training and education.

(Taylor, 2015, p 141)

Or

One initiative which aims to help young adults with a diagnosed mental illness settle into accommodation is the Early Support and Intervention Programme. This programme aims to: help young people manage and keep their tenancies; improve young peoples' living skills, eg budgeting, home and self-care; support community integration; and promote access to employment, training and education.

3)

Some elderly service users remain mobile through activities such as driving or playing golf; others are largely sedentary, spending a lot of time indoors reading or watching TV.

Or

Some elderly service users remain mobile; others are largely sedentary. The former group stay mobile through activities such as driving or playing golf; the latter group spend a lot of time indoors reading or watching TV.

4)

Musson (2017) identifies four main theories of explanation social workers draw upon: psychodynamic, behaviourist, systems and radical.

Chapter 5
Proofreading practice, Task (pages 112–13)

A

Social workers have a generic knowledge and skills base. Traditionally, BA Social Work programmes run for three years and MA programmes for two years.

However, there are now alternative routes to qualification. Social workers can now qualify via fast track or higher apprenticeship programmes.

B

Of central importance to cognitive psychologists is the 'schema' notion. A schema is a mental 'template' that guides behaviour or thought, in a similar way that a recipe is a template for creating an exotic dish. (Schemata actually guide external and external action, external action being observable behaviour, internal action being thought.) Any action, internal or external, will have a schema underpinning it.

Thus, there are schemata for skilled tasks, like driving or typing, schemata for making judgements about people, schemata for language, schemata for perceiving, and so on. Some aspects of certain schemata may be inherited (indeed, the simplest schemata are mere reflex actions); the vast majority are acquired. To those familiar with computers, a schema is little more than the software that drives our action. However, unlike computer software, schemata can replicate, change and become redundant as we experience the world.

Schemata help us process the vast amount of information in the world. They serve us well for the majority of the time; however, they are not always applicable to a particular situation and when we misapply them, errors occur. For example, when we misapply a 'braking' schema whilst driving, we might be involved in an accident. Similarly, the misapplication of 'judgemental' schemata can lead to the creation of stereotypes.

Index

Note: *italicised* page numbers are illustrations, **bold** page numbers are tables.